FAMILIAR
LONDON

▪ MEMORIES OF TIMES PAST ▪

▪ 61 PAINTINGS BY ROSE BARTON ▪

INTRODUCTION BY MARY ANNE EVANS

TEXT BY COLIN INMAN, DAVID BOYLE,
MARY ANNE EVANS AND SUSIE GREEN

A NOTE TO THE READER
In order to keep the pages of the book as uncluttered as possible,
all sources, notes and captions relating to illustrations other than
the main paintings have been grouped at the end of the book, and
will be found on pages 167–169.

The endpapers are taken from a map of 1904 produced by
John Bartholomew and Co. of Edinburgh

First published in the UK in 2006 by Worth Press Ltd, Cambridge, United Kingdom
Reprinted with changes 2008

Mary Anne Evans, Colin Inman, David Boyle and Susie Green have asserted their rights
under the Copyright and Patents Act 1988 to be identified as the authors of the book

Project manager   John Button
Design managers   Lucy Guenot and Catherine Smith

Set in Centaur and Gill Sans by Bookcraft Ltd, Stroud, Gloucestershire
Printed in China by Imago

A Memories of Times Past title
www.memoriesoftimespast.com

ISBN 978 1 903025 45 1

CONTENTS

LONDON: AN IMPERIAL CAPITAL

MARY ANNE EVANS

The Coronation at Westminster Abbey.

In the 1900s, London was the heart of one of the greatest empires the world had known, and, it was fondly believed, one on which the sun would never set. Basking in self-confidence, British citizens were happily indifferent to what was happening in the rest of the world. Events in Russia, the increasingly aggressive stance of the German kaiser, even the historic Anglo-French *entente cordiale* were merely items noted over breakfast in the daily newspapers and then forgotten as the more pressing events of everyday life took over.

Few clouds disturbed the domestic horizon. Home rule for Ireland was not yet an issue, and the suffragette movement—formed in 1903 as the Women's Social and Political Union under the formidable leadership of Emmeline Pankhurst—was in its peaceful infancy. The king had smoothly taken over the monarchy from his much-loved and extremely long-lived mother, Queen Victoria, and was a popular figure. At the start of the king's reign, Henry James had nicknamed him "Edward the Caresser," but he was more affectionately known as "good old Teddy." His peccadilloes and love affairs were tolerated or ignored to the extent that the prominent social life of his mistress, Alice Keppel, was reported in newspaper society columns with no mention made of the king at all.

Life was good, and after a century of industrial progress and the production of vast wealth, London had come to outrival all other cities, drawing visitors from all over Britain and the rest of the world.

Edward VII's coronation in August 1902, from a coronation souvenir that was produced "with the compliments of R. W. Righton, Wholesale, Retail and General Draper, Manchester House, Evesham."

STEAMING INTO LONDON

A visitor's first impressions were bewildering, and those who arrived by train were startled by the sheer sprawl of London. Where did the countryside end and the suburbs begin, they wondered. Where did those suburbs end and "central London" start? In 1905, the population of London had reached the substantial figure of four and a half million but already the middle classes were fleeing to comfortable, neat suburbs like Clapham and Golders Green and even to lower-middle-class Holloway—where George and Weedon Grossmith placed the Pooter family in *Diary of a Nobody*. Throughout the 1900s, London continued to creep farther out—to Hounslow, to Kingston, to Mill Hill and beyond. London was neither like the well-planned, imposing capital of France, nor did it awe the visitor with its ancient glories as did Athens. Instead, the visitor's first view of one of the world's foremost cities was an endless parade of street upon street of two- or three-story redbrick houses, main streets, and shops.

But steaming into the city, all such impressions were put aside. The major railway stations, conveniently close to the West End or the City, were marvels of Victorian engineering, and attached to every major terminus was an equally splendid station hotel. As expensive as these grand hotels might have been, they were definitely the last word in style and modern convenience. The Great Western Hotel beside Paddington, opened in 1854, offered 103 bedrooms and fifteen sitting rooms. Even more impressive was the ornately Gothic Midland Grand Hotel that was attached to St. Pancras Station. It had been designed by the architect of the gilded Albert Memorial, Sir George Gilbert Scott, and boasted a staircase that ascended the whole height of

A photochrome of the Great Western Hotel at Paddington (above). Highgate (right), as painted by the artist John Fulleylove, who lived in Hampstead and died in May 1908.

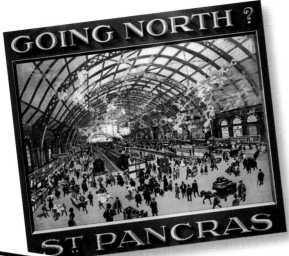

HORSE-DRAWN CARRIAGE OR MOTOR VEHICLE?

Although the Victorian age was known for its great railway projects, the Edwardians were noted for developing other forms of transportation. Society was becoming mobile in a way that transformed the landscape of Britain. Speculative builders invested in suburban housing, enabling the likes of Pooter to move their families to addresses such as "The Laurels" at 12 Brickfield Terrace in Holloway and, neatly rolled umbrellas in hand, commute daily by bus to jobs in the city.

Rose Barton's delightful pictures of central London show peaceful streets full of hansom cabs and horse-drawn carriages taking their passengers up Ludgate Hill toward St. Paul's Cathedral, along the Brompton

The advertisement for the Bedford Hotel comes from *Ryman's Handy Handbook of London*, which boasted more than a hundred illustrations, maps, and cab tariffs and twenty-five theater seating plans. It sold for sixpence. The drawing (below) of a hansom carriage is by Hugh Thomson and was published by Macmillan in 1902 in *Highways and Byways in London*.

the building with cast-iron treads, stone vaulting, and painted walls. The main suites were on the first few floors, the servants' quarters on the top floor, and a gracious ladies' smoking room overlooked Euston Road.

By 1904, even more modest hotels offered such comforts. The Bedford Hotel in Southampton Row, rebuilt in 1900, advertised that it was "heated throughout by radiators," and also boasted electric lights, lifts, baths, three billiard tables, and a conservatory. Room, breakfast, and attendance was five shillings a night. Anyone staying for longer could choose an establishment like the "High Class Residential Mansion facing Regent's Park," which took paying guests at £2, 12 shillings, sixpence a week. It offered "Handsome Reception Rooms, a Billiard Room (full-sized table), Bath room (good sanitary arrangements), Large Garden and Tennis Lawn, Good Cuisine, and Liberal Table," and was to be found in Clarence Gate.

Road and through the parks. And for much of the early Edwardian years, horse-drawn carriages continued to rule the road.

The aristocracy in its elegant landaus and barouches, heraldic arms emblazoned on the side, was still a sight to be seen as the wealthy swept out of the driveways of their grand houses on visits to friends and acquaintances.

For the ordinary public, there were huge numbers of horse-drawn buses and hansom cabs—both two- and four-wheeled—to carry them through the crowded streets. The cabbies came in each day from the poorer East End and worked long hours away from home but, like many professions, they were a close-knit bunch and well looked after. They could eat, drink "harmless beverages," smoke, and read the newspapers in between fares at any of the forty-five small wooden buildings erected in the middle of the roads and provided by the Cabman's Shelter Fund. In their old age, the Cab-drivers Benevolent Association supported the likes of Knock Softly, Crimea Sailor Jack, and Little Hill, each of whom had spent over forty years "on the box."

But cabbies were a disappearing breed, and in the early years of the century, the introduction of new vehicles of all kinds threatened their way of life. By 1903, taxis,

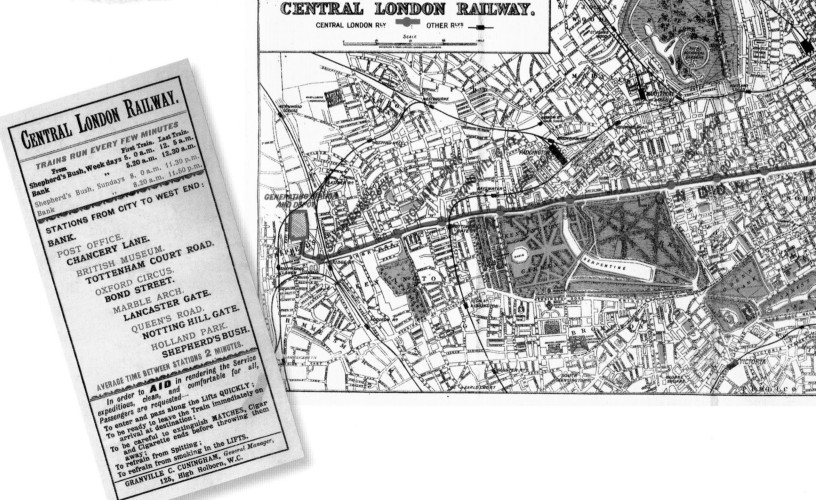

buses, and electric streetcars had all appeared on the roads, challenging the older forms of transportation. At first noisy and prone to breaking down, the mechanical vehicles were constantly improving and, much to the disgust of the original cabbies, were able to cut the fares to sixpence a mile.

By 1904, subways were taking the public to more places and the whole of London, from Islington to Clapham Common, from Finsbury Park to Moorgate, was becoming accessible. The Metropolitan District Railway, the world's first underground passenger railway, had been operating since 1860 but it was crowded, uncomfortable, and lit by gas lamps. The Central Line,

which opened in 1900, pointed the way to the future. It was the first completely electric underground railway and by 1903 carried up to 140,000 passengers a day from Bank to Shepherd's Bush. There was big money to be made in transportation and speculators rushed to invest. The network grew rapidly, and with the Baker Street and Waterloo ("Bakerloo") and Piccadilly and Brompton lines, both of which opened in 1906, the modern underground system was in place.

But it was the introduction of the automobile that was to change traveling habits forever. At first, the newfangled vehicle was feared and disliked by many, from the cabbies with their vulnerable horse-drawn vehicles to such eccentric individuals as the Marquess of Queensbury who, when applying for a gun license, pointed out that he needed it to shoot the motorists who drove through his estate.

There was good reason to worry. By 1904, an estimated 8,465 automobiles had taken to the roads. The world was moving faster, and the statutory speed limit was raised from 14 mph to a fearsomely fast 20 mph throughout England, though in 1904 the Royal Parks authority restricted the limit within the city's

This automobile (above) was photographed in color and then printed from three process plates by John Swain and Sons on Farringdon Street; it was featured in the *Penrose Pictorial Annual* for 1902–3.

The Central London Railway (left) advertised "workmen's tickets," available on weekdays before 7:00 a.m. at twopence for a return fare, or a book of twenty-four tickets could be bought from any station for four shillings.

parks to the stately and far more appropriate 10 mph. By 1910, boosted by the introduction of the Model T Ford from the United States, the number had grown to 53,196. The automobile was here to stay.

A BUILDING FRENZY

It was not only the needs of the developing transportation system that caused roads to be dug up for streetcar lines and cavernous tunnels to be built for the subway. Everywhere, it seemed, hundreds of old buildings were being torn down in the name of progress.

In 1904, the last and one of the greatest—and most disruptive—of the Victorian metropolitan improvements was nearing completion. The Kingsway and Aldwych scheme, which began in 1900, had cleared the streets north of the Strand, opposite Somerset House, a grand building curtly dismissed in Thomas Cook's 1904 *Handbook for London* as "devoted to inland revenue, wills, etc." The improvements, designed to create a business area to rival the City of London, cost around £5 million and covered twenty-eight acres. The opening of Kingsway in October 1905 by Edward VII, after whom it was named, was a splendid occasion.

The prevailing taste in architecture, like many other aspects of Edwardian life, ran to flamboyance and ornate decoration, and many of London's flat-fronted, dark, eighteenth-century houses were being given rich new frontages and equally opulent interiors. At the southern end of Mayfair, Piccadilly was being transformed on the Green Park side with new banks and offices, restaurants, and shops. In 1904, the outlines of César Ritz's great hotel, the first major steel-framed building in London, appeared, and across the road cranes crowded the skyline in preparation for the construction of Norman Shaw's grand Piccadilly Hotel.

Philip Norman painted *Holywell Street Looking East* (above) in 1900. This street, full of secondhand bookshops, was destroyed in the construction work to create Kingsway. The steeple of the church of St. Clement Dane is visible at the end of the street, as it is in the drawing (right) of workmen by Hugh Thomson entitled *When the Strand Is Up*, dated 1902.

THE CAREFREE LIFE OF
THE UPPER CLASSES

Against such a frenzy and desire for change, social mores for those at the top of the tree remained comfortingly fixed. The king led the way with his personal circle of friends, known as the "Marlborough Set," to which a privileged few gained access, while about 600 prominent London families provided the basis of high society.

The immense wealth of London's aristocracy was evident in the town houses that graced Park Lane, Mayfair, and St. James's. "Mansions of the nobility" were deemed important enough to warrant a separate section in Thomas Cook's 1904 *Handbook for London*, which guided visitors to addresses like Apsley House,

owned by the Duke of Wellington; Devonshire House, home of the Duchess of Devonshire; the Duke of Westminster's Grosvenor House; and that "splendid specimen of architecture, created at a cost of £250,000," Stafford House on the Mall (now called Lancaster House), the home of the Duke of Sutherland. It had always been a grand building, indeed so grand that Queen Victoria, a frequent visitor, had once dryly remarked to her friend, the second duke's wife, "I have come from my house to your palace."

Pomp and circumstance, flamboyance, and excess—at least for the upper classes—ruled as they enthusiastically adopted Oscar Wilde's notion that "nothing succeeds like excess" as the mantra of their time. With income tax at sixpence in the pound, the

Gold Cup Day at Ascot (above) in June was attended by the king and queen. Then, as now, it was the highlight of the racing season and was a chance for people to show off the latest fashions.

The Midnight Ball at the Savoy Hotel (above), featured in a brochure entitled "London's Social Calendar," presented to patrons of the Savoy Hotel in about 1906. This same brochure shows the painting (right) captioned "Dining at the Berkeley." The photo (below) shows the ballroom at Devonshire House as published in the Penrose Pictorial Annual of 1903–4.

same as the price of the ladies' weekly newspaper *The Queen*, the rich could afford to indulge themselves as much as they pleased. Life was an endless round of pleasure, organized into a fixed pattern that kept society amused from the moment the maid opened the curtains and lit the bedroom fire to the last after-dinner cigar of a long evening.

The London summer season ran from after Easter to the races at Ascot in late June, with the smart set returning to the capital for a week or so at Christmas. "London society was brilliant," wrote Princess Marie Louise in *My Memories of Six Reigns*. "Balls, receptions and of course large dinner parties took place every evening, and it was quite a usual occurrence to go to more than one ball the same night . . . There was no necessity to entertain outside one's own friends' houses, as

in those days the Dorchester House, Grosvenor House, Lansdowne House, Derby House, Stafford House—all these beautiful residences were still inhabited by their owners." They remained in private ownership until 1914, when that world of privilege was swept away.

A DRESS FOR EVERY OCCASION

Conspicuous consumption was seen as desirable and nowhere was it more conspicuous—or more desirable—than in female attire. Society ladies were elaborately dressed, changing frequently throughout the day, as each social occasion demanded a different costume. Well-dressed Edwardian women were slaves to fashion, which in the 1900s took the shape of the S figure, the hourglass shape that gave the buxom appearance so admired by Edward VII. Carrying it off was not so easy, however, and the tightly restricted waist caused many women to faint in public, particularly at long and elaborate dinner parties where an indigestible twelve large courses were the norm. But when successful, the

DRESSMAKERS PREFER TO FIT OVER
ROYAL WORCESTER KIDFITTING CORSETS,
WHICH GIVE THE BEST DRESS EFFECTS.

Oxford Street; and Gamages in Holborn—all had started out as Victorian dealers in cloth or accessories but had seized on clothing as a far more profitable source of revenue after the invention of industrial sewing machines and mass production.

Gentlemen continued to favor custom tailors, and relied on Savile Row for their suits and St. James's for hats, shoes, and shirts. Provisions for the wealthy came from their respected grocer Fortnum & Mason, founded way back in 1705 on St. James's, and from Harrods, which from 1901 to 1905 was expanding into the huge and familiar red terra-cotta building at Knightsbridge. Hatchards, operating since 1797 in Piccadilly, continued to supply books to the discerning—and to the royal family when they went on vacation.

These marvelous hats (above) were made out of Dennison's imperial crêpe paper; images of them were printed using the Zander process in the *Penrose Pictorial Annual* of 1906–7.

effect was impressive. In *Goodbye Piccadilly*, W. McQueen Pope enthused, "The sight of an Edwardian lady, stepping out of her Brougham, her Victoria or Landau outside a Regent Street shop was a spectacle . . . The lady swept across the pavement like a Queen, like a procession of one, for she knew how to move and carry herself. She had balance and poise, she had elegance and she was one hundred per cent feminine. She paid no attention to the world around, to the envious glances of her less favoured sisters, but she proceeded like a ship in full sail, a gracious galleon into the harbour of the favoured emporium."

Ladies bought their dresses from court dressmakers, from French designers in Paris like Worth and, increasingly in the early 1900s, from a favorite London emporium. Stores like Debenham & Freebody at 44 Wigmore Street; Liberty & Co. (known for Asian goods of all kinds), Swan & Edgar, and Dickins & Jones, all on Regent Street; Marshall & Snelgrove on

One of the Sights of London.
Famous for over a Century for Taste, for Quality, for Value.

DEBENHAM
AND
FREEBODY.
Established 1795.

WIGMORE STREET AND
WELBECK STREET, CAVEN-
DISH SQUARE, LONDON, W.

TWO MINUTES FROM OXFORD STREET
AND BOND STREET (NORTH END).

EVERY ARTICLE OF FEMININE ATTIRE OF
THE HIGHEST QUALITY KEPT IN STOCK.

Retail was a cutthroat business but the profits were enormous, and retailers were invariably the most enthusiastic supporters of any new technology that might give them an edge over their rivals. Harrods had installed the first escalator in London in 1898, wisely placing an assistant at the top to revive the nervous with smelling salts and brandy. William Whiteley, who in 1872 billed himself as the "Universal Provider" and offered to supply anything "from a pin to an elephant at short notice," had gone further than his fellow shopkeepers by breaking the agreed retail demarcations that existed: he was the first to sell far more than accessories. Soon after, Gamages in Holborn, the self-styled "People's Popular Emporium," offered accessories, furniture, and gardening, sports, and camping equipment as well as clothing (Gamages was the official outfitter of the Boy Scouts). With an eye to the main chance, the ever-resourceful Arthur Gamage added a zoological section, a toy department, and in 1903 an automotive department. Moving with the times, he brought in mail-order catalogs for bicycles, motorcycles, and cycling equipment. This profitable department was such a favorite of the innovative, if eccentric, retailer that he chose it as the location for his funeral.

Many of Gamage's ideas (though not that of the funeral) were adopted by the man who made the greatest impact on Edwardian London's shopping habits, the American Gordon Selfridge. Backed by Sam Waring of Waring & Gillow on the condition that he not sell furniture, a promise that Selfridge always kept, he bought the land for his store on Oxford Street in 1906 and opened the doors three years later. Selfridges caused a huge sensation with its wide range of goods and its giant Ionic architectural style—designed by Daniel Burnham of Chicago, where the young Selfridge had first worked.

Gordon Selfridge and his fellow retailers had created emporia that were different from the small, cramped, individual, and limited shops lining the high streets of the suburbs. Large plate-glass windows gave passersby a seductive glimpse into a glittering interior where the goods were prominently displayed—along with the prices. Stepping through the generous mahogany and brass doors gave a sense of occasion and, once inside, the most modern electric lighting and spacious layout made shopping for tea gowns, ball gowns, ostrich-feathered hats, gloves, and shoes an altogether glamorous expedition.

The announcement of the opening of Selfridges (top) was reproduced in the *Penrose Pictorial Annual* of 1909–10. It accompanied an article describing these advertisements (which were printed on full pages in newspapers and illustrated by well-known artists such as Walter Crane) as a major event in pictorial publicity. The Tuck's postcard (above) shows the costume salon at Harrods. The drawing by Hugh Thomson (right) is dated 1899, and shows shoppers in Regent Street. The advertisement for Gamages (top right) comes from the January 1905 edition of *Chums* magazine.

WHAT LONDON SIGHTS
THERE ARE TO SEE

There was little point to such finery unless it was paraded for all to see, in public as well as at private balls and dinners. During London's social season, Rotten Row was, as Rose Barton depicts in her colorful scenes, the haunt of fashion. Elegant young ladies mounted sidesaddle with a liveried groom in attendance, the rich and the glamorous—all rode or walked through the park daily while the onlookers stood

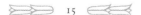

respectfully on the other side of the railings watching the peacock parade pass by. It was part of the daily social round for everyone, and anything remarkable—the height of a lady's feather in her hat, the unusual color of a gown—was duly reported the next day in the *Daily Graphic* or on the society pages of the more respectable publications.

Members of the royal family were more difficult to spot but, happily for the curious, there were enough buildings to stand outside in the hopes of a glimpse of a royal personage. Buckingham Palace was closed to the public, but the neighboring Royal Mews could be viewed on application by letter to the Crown Equerry. The colorful military band of the Foot Guards played daily at 10:40 a.m. in Marlborough Court Quadrangle outside St. James's Palace, moving to Buckingham Palace when the king was in residence, while the changing of the guard took place daily at Horse Guards at 11:00 a.m. The State Apartments at Kensington Palace, birthplace of Queen Victoria, were open to the public, as was Hampton Court Palace and Windsor Castle, where the entry charge of one shilling for adults and sixpence for children on certain weekdays was given to local charities. Royal sightseeing in Edwardian times was very much like it is today.

The first-time visitor could book a guided tour of the town with one of "Cook's Drives in London,

The Henley Regatta (center left), as portrayed in the Savoy Hotel social calendar. The morning promenade in Kensington Gardens (below left), also from the social calendar of 1906.

Accompanied by a Competent Guide," which went every weekday from 10:00 a.m. to 5:30 p.m. from Cook's Reading and Waiting Room in Ludgate Circus. Cook's Ludgate Circus offices were a tourist attraction in their own right. They were extremely lavish, with dressing rooms, lavatories, and full ticketing facilities. Here, overseas tourists could rest awhile and read the newspapers while waiting to buy coupons for accommodation at different London hotels, ranging from seven shillings, sixpence to ten shillings, sixpence per night. They could have their letters addressed and mailed to any part of the globe, and purchase the popular and indispensable Cook's *Handbook for London*, which was reissued every year.

Handbook in hand, the intrepid do-it-yourself visitor followed a well-trodden route, marveling at the Bank of England from the internal courtyard that was open to all; visiting the chapel of Chelsea Hospital, hung with dusty, decaying banners from the wars that had helped make the British empire great; and applying to the porter of the Mansion House to see the Lord Mayor's splendid State Apartments. In between such exhausting sightseeing and, of course, shopping, a reviving cup of tea in a Lyons' Corner House or an "A.B.C. tea shop" (the rather more acceptable name for the Aerated Bread Company's tearooms) was most welcome. At the end of the day, there was the pleasure of eating in one of London's many restaurants—perhaps a shellfish dinner at Scott's Oyster and Supper Rooms in Coventry Street or a meal at the Holborn Restaurant, which advertised the added attraction of "high class instrumental music."

A PASSION FOR THE STAGE

One particular passion was shared by all classes of society—the theater, which occupied the place in Edwardian times that films do today. In the top West End theaters, the best stall seats cost ten shillings, sixpence, but prices for the "galleryites" and the "pittites" varied from one shilling to two shillings, sixpence respectively. While everyone flocked to see the latest work by Arthur Wing Pinero, the wealthy enjoyed a standard of comfort not shared by the less well-off: some of the older theaters employed "packers" to push as many people as possible into the cheaper seats, hard wooden benches that had neither cushions nor physical divisions between onlookers.

In addition to the many theaters that were already well established, more were built in the 1900s, like the Apollo, Criterion, and Haymarket. The theater that elicited the most admiring comments was opened in 1904. The Coliseum, designed by Frank Matcham and owned by Oswald Stoll, incorporated a three-section moving stage and a revolving, electrically lit advertising globe on the roof. There were telephones, a messenger

service, a pillar-shaped box for mail, a garden restaurant, elevators, and even a mobile royal lounge that took the royal guests down into the reception foyer from the first floor.

Away from the city center, the working class of London had their own music halls and theaters—establishments like the Metropole in Camberwell, the Britannia in Hoxton, the Grand in Islington, and the Pavilion in Whitechapel. The latter was so imposing it was dubbed, inevitably, "the Drury Lane of the East."

With such a choice of entertainment, the customer could afford to be hugely critical, and competition was fierce as theaters vied with each other in an effort to gain reputations and loyal audiences. At the Duke of York's, American Charles Frohman made a name for himself by bringing leading actors and actresses from his home country to the London stage. He also put on the first performances of J. M. Barrie's *Peter Pan* in December 1904. It was a success from the start, captivating grown-ups, children, and critics alike, and even the often-acerbic newspaper *The Stage* was moved to write that *Peter Pan* was "a piece that no-one, old or young, should resist." It starred Nina Boucicault as Peter and Gerald du Maurier as both Mr. Darling and Captain Hook, and it ran for 145 performances. The Gaiety Theatre in the Strand—rebuilt in 1904 with 1,338 seats as part of the new Kingsway scheme—put on musicals, but it was better known for the Gaiety Girls and their admirers, the Stage Door Johnnies, who could offer a respectable entrée into aristocratic society. Baroness Cheniston, Countess Dowlett, and the Countess of Drogheda all came from the ranks of the glamorous and popular Gaiety Girls.

Even by the somewhat extravagant standards of the time, the Theatre Royal in Drury Lane was famous for its spectacular drama, complete with earthquakes, snowstorms, shipwrecks, and horse races. Even the occasional elephant made a stage appearance. Dan Leno, originally a music hall star who successfully made the crossover into theater, appeared annually in pantomimes, and Dame Ellen Terry celebrated her stage jubilee there in June 1905.

A private box party at the Covent Garden Theatre (left), from the Savoy Hotel social calendar. The Japanese-born painter Yoshio Markino painted the Strand's New Gaiety Theatre (right). Hugh Thomson drew the crowd to *Gods* in 1899 (center).

Others would never forget the continuous noise that assaulted the senses—the sound of horses' hooves, the screech of streetcar wheels against metal tracks, the cries of the street vendors, and the hoarse voices of the newspaper boys advertising the dailies with shouts of "Spay-shul!" or "Orl the Winners."

And what visitor who had come to London in 1904 would forget his first visit to the gleaming cast-iron and glass exhibition hall of the Royal Horticultural Society, which opened with such fanfare on July 22, or the London Symphony Orchestra's first performance on June 9 in the Queen's Hall in Langham Place?

Spectacles of another kind were provided by the actor-manager Sir Herbert (Beerbohm) Tree, whose productions of Shakespeare's plays were fanciful to say the least. Imagine this setting in *A Winter's Tale*: "The Sicilian and Bohemian courts where fumes of incense curl round golden statues of Apollo, and white-coated priests chant ancient dirges, and helmets flash and bare-armed maidens hover round golden couches—these are wonders of design." They may seem over the top today, but such dramatic devices were beloved by Edwardian audiences, and Tree packed His Majesty's Theatre nightly with his Shakespearian extravaganzas.

A FOND FAREWELL TO LONDON

Waiting for trunks to be collected from the hotel and taken back to the railway station for the long journey home, what images of London would be uppermost in an Edwardian visitor's mind?

Each person's impression would have been personal and different. Some might have been entranced by London's unexpectedly colorful street life—the green grass and plane trees of the royal parks and the private squares glimpsed from the open top of a bus, the cheerful pinks and greens of flowers wrapped up in vivid blue paper by the flower sellers in Piccadilly Circus, and the yellow hay from horses' feed blowing along the pavement.

That initial view of endless, uniform suburbs was banished by the excitement of a city that seemed to reinvent itself daily. No other capital appeared both so culturally rich and so teeming with such a bewildering diversity of everyday sights and sounds. London life was a rich experience.

To the visitor from Hamburg or New York, the commuter from Kingston and the young debutante up from the country for her first social season, London was irresistible. Life was to change irrevocably with the outbreak of war in 1914, when the world was torn apart and a whole generation of those young men, who had danced their careless way through the early years of the century, was wiped out. But that was ten years hence, and in 1904 London still basked in the long and sunlit afternoon of the Edwardian era.

ROSE BARTON
1856–1929

COLIN INMAN

April 21st 1907:

Rose Barton was born in Ireland on April 21, 1856. Her father was Augustine Barton of Rochestown, near Cahir in County Tipperary. He lived the life of a country gentleman, although he was nominally listed as a solicitor. In his youth, he was sent abroad for the

sake of his health and spent some time in Australia, where he managed to invest and lose a fortune of £10,000, returning home with only a case of butterflies, a gold nugget, and a "Red Indian" costume. While wearing this at a fancy dress ball, he managed to captivate Mrs. James McCalmont, a widow who was born Emily Martin. After their marriage in 1853, she became known in the family as "Mrs. B."

In 1881, Rose's elder sister Emily Alma married George Frederick Brooke, who became a baronet in 1903. Most of the couple's ten children seem to have had warlike inclinations, and made careers in various regiments, but Raymond Brooke, born in 1885, took over the family wine business and in 1961 wrote a history of the family, rather more lively than most of its type, called *The Brimming River* (published by Allen Figgis of Dublin). It is in this book that occasional snippets of information about Aunt Rose, as she was known, can be found. Its cover carries a watercolor by Rose, probably of a Dublin street.

Among Rose's other relatives was her cousin Edith Somerville, the artist and writer best known as the joint author of *Some Experiences of an Irish R.M.*

Rose and Emily were educated at home, as befitted young ladies from such a background. They had a German governess, were taught drawing, and learned to play the piano. As babies, according to Brooke, Mrs. B fed them Guinness stout, as she believed it was good for the complexion.

A letter from a Dublin address signed by Rose Barton (above). It almost certainly refers to the proceeds of playing cards!

A drawing of Rose Barton (left), embarking on a fishing expedition, dated April 21, 1907. This is the only known portrait of the artist.

College Green, Dublin (right) was painted in 1887. It is not clear when Rose Barton painted *A Quiet Harbour at Dusk* (below), but *A Sunny Cornfield* (below right) was painted in 1887.

The girls were presented at court in 1872 and underwent the usual season of dinner parties, dances, private theatricals, and hunt balls. Rose is reported as having done a certain amount of hunting. However, Augustine Barton died in 1874, and the following winter his widow took the two daughters to Brussels, where they had drawing and painting lessons. They then traveled up the Rhine for an extended stay in Switzerland.

Soon afterward, Brookes writes, Rose had an unfortunate love affair with a young man who was heavily in debt. It is tempting to wonder whether the love affair was the precursor to the long continental trip rather than, as he suggests, following it. However, Aunt Rose never saw the young man again, as he contracted "some type of fever" and died within six months. Rose then decided to concentrate professionally on her painting, which she did until well into the 1920s, exhibiting widely and holding "several very successful one-man shows of her own."

One of Rose's contemporaries in the 1870s was Mildred Anne Butler (1858–1941) from nearby Kilmurry, and their families jointly decided to send Mildred and Rose to study art in Paris with Henri Gervex, a salon painter who ran a successful teaching studio. She also studied in London under Paul Naftel. She first exhibited in Dublin in 1878 at the Royal Hibernian Academy, and in London appeared at the Dudley Gallery and the Society of Lady Artists in 1880. She continued to divide her time between Dublin and London before finally moving in 1903 to 79 Park Mansions, Knightsbridge, where she lived until her death.

Rose Barton was elected as an associate member of the Society of Lady Artists in 1886 and of the Royal Society of Painters in Water-Colours (RWS) in 1893, although she was not elected to full membership until 1911.

Her first important show was at the Japanese Gallery on New Bond Street in 1893, where she showed sixty paintings of London, presumably including many of those subsequently published in *Familiar London*.

St. Auden's Arch (top left), *Kildare Street Club and Nassan Street* (top right), and *A Narrow Lane with a Peep of Church Street* (bottom right) were published in Gerard's *Picturesque Dublin Old and New*, the only other book illustrated by Rose Barton. *An Evening on the River Liffey with St. John's Church in the Distance* (bottom left) was painted in 1905.

Contemporary commentators compared her work to that of Herbert Marshall, who illustrated A&C Black's *The Scenery of London*, published in 1905. She was also praised for her depiction of a London fog, a phenomenon that she admitted in her book held great attraction for her.

In 1898, Rose Barton provided the illustrations for Francis Gerard's *Picturesque Dublin Old and New*. This included ninety-one gray-wash drawings of the city, reproduced in monochrome.

A far more comprehensive portrayal of her work came with *Familiar London*, published by A&C Black in 1904, which reproduced sixty-one of her paintings in color. She also wrote the text for the book. Sales were obviously disappointing for it was never reprinted, and no other books bearing her sole name as illustrator were published, although A&C Black included her

illustrations with those of other artists in a number of subsequent books. Although her pictures became increasingly unfashionable over the next twenty years, she continued to exhibit from time to time.

She lived out the rest of her life in Knightsbridge, accompanied by a nurse, and was remembered with affection by her younger relations, most of whom were her sister's children. Raymond Brooke recalls that he and his siblings often spent a day with Aunt Rose in London when traveling to or from their schools. On one occasion at the zoo, Brooke writes, "there was a monkey which for some reason detested women and there was a notice on the cage to the effect that he was on no account to be annoyed. Aunt Rose stood in front of the cage and opened her umbrella, whereupon the monkey

flew into a rage, made balls of the sawdust in his cage and hurled them at her. She was in those days, as indeed to the end of her life, the most delightful companion." And it would seem, a somewhat friskier one than might have been expected of a maiden aunt.

Among the skills taught her in youth were a proficiency at playing whist. She later enjoyed piquet and also played bridge to the end of her life. She was a good backgammon player, often winning money from unsuspecting younger opponents. She bet on horse races, and Raymond Brooke recalls that, as her executor, he had to pay her bookie £3 on the Monday after her death. Affected by asthma in her later years, Rose Barton died at home in Knightsbridge on October 10, 1929.

Much of the factual information about her life is speculative, but debt must be paid to articles by Charles Nugent of Christie's watercolor department and

Rebecca Rowe in the catalog of an exhibition of Rose Barton's paintings held in Ireland and London in 1987. This exhibition, which included many of the pictures used to illustrate *Familiar London*, helped reawaken interest in her work, as did the sale of paintings by Christie's at Elveden Hall in 1984, including many of those formerly owned by Lord Iveagh, a family friend.

In recent years, the few of her paintings that have come up at auction have sold for unexpectedly large sums. In December 2005, a watercolor that spent decades hanging in a garden shed fetched £8,800 at an auction in Gloucestershire. The foggy winter cityscape, with children walking in a park, had been hanging in the sellers' shed for as long as they could remember. The highest price to date for a Rose Barton painting— £17,000—was achieved in 1999 when Sotheby's sold a charming watercolor of a little girl.

The atmospheric painting of Westminster Abbey (top left) is not dated; *Hyde Park Corner with the Household Cavalry on a Rainy Day* (top right) was painted in 1918.

PLATE 1

H.R.H. PRINCE GEORGE OF WALES WATCHING THE SCOTS GUARDS FROM MARLBOROUGH HOUSE

The Household Troops in their dashing scarlet uniforms are still a familiar sight.

Rose Barton's romantic painting is of the two-year-old Prince George Edward, the fifth child of the future George V (Edward VII's son). His original titles included Prince of Saxe-Coburg and Gotha and Duke of Saxony, but these were discontinued in 1917. He became Duke of Kent, the Earl of St. Andrews, and Baron Downpatrick in 1934. Here he sits on a wall of Marlborough House, which was built between 1709 and 1711 for Sarah, Duchess of Marlborough. A royal residence for almost 250 years, it is now a Commonwealth Centre for the British government, but the gravestones of the dogs Muff, Tiny, and Joss, and of Benny the Bunny, the deceased pets of Queen Alexandra, who lived there from 1910 to 1925 after Edward VII's death, still remain in the garden.

The young prince, entranced, watches the Scots Guards parading below him. Originally formed by Charles I in 1642 specifically to quell a rebellion by the Irish, who were resentful

of the Scots colonizing Ulster, they have always had a close link with the sovereign. Charles I originally intended to go to Ulster, and the Scots were to have been his Royal Guard. Now they are one of the Household Troops whose honor it is to protect the sovereign. This historic battalion may be seen every fifth year "trooping the color" on Horse Guards Parade, Whitehall, before receiving the monarch's personal salute. Recently, the Scots Guards served in Iraq; they returned in May 2005.

PLATE 2

WESTMINSTER

Following its destruction by fire in 1834, the Palace of Westminster was rebuilt
in the Gothic style to the design of architect Sir Charles Barry.

The Clock Tower—generally but inaccurately called Big Ben—was one of the last parts of the Palace of Westminster to be completed, in 1858. The name Big Ben actually belongs to the bell that, along with the clock, came into use the following year. The clock is set in a framework 23 feet in diameter; the minute hand is 14 feet long and the figures are 2 feet high. Big Ben itself weighs over 13 tons. Who Ben was remains uncertain. One theory has it that he was Sir Benjamin Hall, the Chief Commissioner of Works. Another theory gives the name to one Benjamin Caunt, a popular contemporary amateur boxer who was the publican of the Coach and Horses in St. Martin's Lane and who weighed 250 pounds.

The annual ceremony of the State Opening of Parliament dates back to the opening of the rebuilt Palace of Westminster in 1852. Edward VII—always conscious of the image of the monarchy—increased the pageantry of the occasion when he became king in 1901, replacing the single throne with a double throne for himself and Queen Alexandra.

Parliament was the focus of the suffragettes' campaign for the right of women to vote. In 1908, protesters smuggled a banner into the Gallery of the House of Commons and unfurled it in front of shocked members of Parliament.

PLATE 3

THE DRIVE, HYDE PARK

From the seventeenth century onward, when kings Charles I and II ensured public access,
the aristocracy and people of fashion came to Hyde Park to show themselves to the world.

In Hyde Park, carriage exercise took place in the Drive where, in 1896, could be seen "unbroken lines of sumptuous equipages drawn by the finest coach-horses money can purchase, and occupied by some of the best dressed and most beautiful women in the world, who drive here at stated hours." Riding or driving in Hyde Park was a major test of etiquette and savoir faire. Members of well-established aristocratic families learned how to ride, and how to dress to ride, from early childhood. Newer entrants to the upper classes—those whose money had been more recently acquired, most likely from business—also had to become polished equestrians, to acquire a decent mount (probably from one of the many stables close to Hyde Park), and to dress themselves and their servants properly.

Ambitious drivers aspired to be admitted to the exclusive Coaching Club, which staged four meetings each year in Hyde Park. These were grand occasions. "Everything was absolutely spick and span," one observer wrote. "The liveries fitted the grooms like gloves, and their cockaded top hats and smart top boots had been respectively brushed and polished until they gleamed and shone like so many mirrors in the sunlight. The colours of the liveries matched the colours of their coaches, dark mahogany, dark blue, dark olive green, maroon, and so on."

PLATE 4

THE ROW

Rotten Row, on the south side of Hyde Park, is said to take its name from *Route du Roi*,
the road taken by William III on his journeys from the court at Kensington Palace to Westminster.

In the late seventeenth century, William III had Rotten Row illuminated with 300 oil lamps to guard against highwaymen and footpads—not wholly successfully, as in 1749 robbers relieved the writer Horace Walpole of his gold watch and eight guineas. In the nineteenth century, and well on into the twentieth, Rotten Row was the place to ride. The 1911 edition of Baedeker's *London* reported that "in the Row are numerous riders, who parade their spirited and glossy steeds before the interested crowd sitting or walking at the sides. On fine Sundays the 'Church Parade,' between morning-service and luncheon . . . is one of the best displays of dress and fashion in London."

The beau monde frequented Rotten Row. So too did the "demi-monde." Dressed and mounted well, high-class prostitutes—popularly known as "horse-breakers"—found plenty of opportunities there. One, a Liverpool girl named Catherine Walters, who rode a chestnut horse, became the mistress of Lord Hartington, heir to the Duke of Devonshire, and also became mistress of a house in Mayfair, with an income of £2,000 per year.

As always, decorum was essential. In 1908, Edward VII became greatly exercised about women who failed to ride sidesaddle in the park. The police and the government were involved. Nothing official could be done to enforce the monarch's wishes—but he had the last word, sending instructions from the royal yacht to "let it be known that ladies who ride astride in the Park will not be allowed to come to Court."

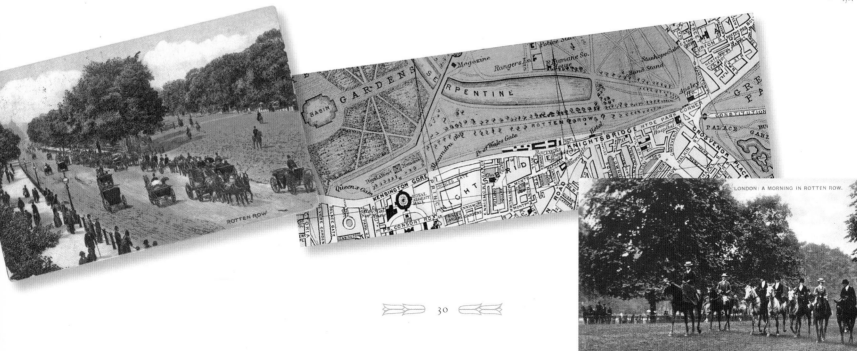

PLATE 5

LUDGATE HILL

Ludgate Hill is one of the three ancient hills of London, the others being Tower Hill and Cornhill.

Ludgate Hill takes its name from Lud Gate, probably built by the Romans as the entrance to one of their major cemeteries in Fleet Street, but traditionally thought to have been built by Lud, king of the Britons in 66 BC. Once a puissant ruler, Lud's statue originally adorned the gate, but now neglected, forlorn and crumbling, resides in a "sordid little niche" in the doorway of St. Dunstan in the West, Fleet Street.

Certainly the Romans' footprint is everywhere in this part of London. When Sir Christopher Wren was rebuilding St. Martin within Ludgate after the Great Fire of 1666, he discovered the tombstone of a Roman legionnaire, Vivius Marciarnus, set up by "his most devoted wife" Januaria Martina. And Wren's masterpiece, St. Paul's Cathedral, is reputedly built on the site of the ancient Roman temple to the lunar goddess of the hunt, Diana.

The railway viaduct was built in 1865 by the London, Chatham and Dover Railway to reach Ludgate Hill Station, the new epicenter for commuters from the then-faraway and leafy suburbs such as Tottenham, Richmond, Enfield, and Crystal Palace. A plaque on the bridge commemorates England's first daily paper, the *Daily Courant*, which was published by Edward Mallett in 1702 from his nearby premises "against the Ditch at Fleet Bridge." Ludgate Hill Station is now closed, like so many other once-useful railway stations.

PLATE 6

GROSVENOR PLACE ON A WET DAY

Since 1677, the Grosvenor family has owned two large estates, one of which
now comprises some of Westminster's prime locations.

Few hospitals, run as they were by the church, had survived the sixteenth-century Reformation in England, so Georgian England saw the building of a plethora of hospitals, founded in a spirit of enlightened philanthropy by the wealthy. One such was the first building on Grosvenor Place, the Lock Hospital for Venereal Diseases (1746), described as being for "females suffering from disorders contracted by a vicious course of life." The building was demolished in 1846, four years after the hospital had moved to the Harrow Road.

George III had bought nearby Buckingham House for £28,000 in 1762, and objected strongly to the Grosvenors building a row of houses that would overlook his grounds. The treasury, however, was unimpressed by his royal distress, and declined to grant him the £20,000 required to buy the land. From 1767 onward, George's privacy was no more. By the mid-nineteenth century, the building of Grosvenor Place was complete and Buckingham Palace, the grandiose replacement for Buckingham House, was finished. This palace, initiated by George IV in 1819, cost a monumental £700,000. It is protected by the wall that runs down the whole of the royal side of Grosvenor Place.

The horse omnibus doggedly making its way through the rain, its bedraggled passengers on the top deck shielding themselves from the elements, was first introduced to London from Paris by George Shillibeer in 1829. Faithful horses last pulled their passengers through London's streets in 1919.

C.42287. LONDON. BUCKINGHAM PALACE.

PLATE 7

UNDER HUNGERFORD BRIDGE

Hungerford Bridge was built to connect the West End's Charing Cross with the south bank of the Thames.

The Hungerford Bridge that Rose Barton painted, running over the Embankment, was the second on the site. A first toll bridge had been built by the great engineer Isambard Kingdom Brunel in the 1840s. For pedestrians only, it linked the old Hungerford fruit and vegetable market—rebuilt in 1833 because the original 1682 market had proved to be inadequate in comparison to Covent Garden—with the south bank of the Thames. Brunel's early bridge was a creative success, being painted by James McNeill Whistler and photographed by William Henry Fox Talbot, but commercially it failed—dismally. This may have been because pedestrians did not want to enter the heavy, obnoxious stink emanating from the polluted Thames, which from time to time drove the members of Parliament out of the Palace of Westminster.

In 1860, Hungerford Market was demolished to make way for the Charing Cross railway station, and Sir John Hawkshaw replaced Brunel's bridge with a nine-span, wrought-iron, lattice railway bridge. Today, running on either side of Hawkshaw's bridge, a foot suspension bridge has risen again, like a phoenix, in a startling contemporary form. The new spectacular footbridge, spanning both sides of the railway bridge, was designed by Alex Lifschutz and Ian Davidson and opened in May 2002.

Rose Barton focuses on the horse-drawn cabs waiting by the roadside to ply their trade. By 1860, there were more than 11,500 cabs, and congestion in London became so intense that the police introduced regulations that forced the cabs to stay on their "rank," as they are here, until someone hired them.

PLATE 8

A HOT AFTERNOON IN PICCADILLY

A cabman waits for hire in prestigious Piccadilly, which in the nineteenth century
had housed luminaries as diverse as Lord Byron and the Duke of York.

Piccadilly was originally a Roman highway leading west out of London, surrounded by countryside. Then, in the early seventeenth century, one Robert Baker, a tailor, made an enormous fortune from a stiff collar known as the "picadil" and used it to buy land north of the area that is now Piccadilly Circus. There he built a great house, which was nicknamed Piccadilly Hall. By the mid-eighteenth century, the highway had become commonly known as Piccadilly.

The snoozing driver, drawn up adjacent to Green Park, seems to be driving an 1836-type cab. An improved version of Joseph Harrison's patented design of 1834, it had a window in its roof, allowing the driver to communicate with his passengers. This driver may have been just drowsy, but being a cabman was a hard job, and in Victorian times these men were known for their equally hard drinking. This cabbie may well have been "sleeping it off." The problem was so widespread that various philanthropists, among them the Earl of Shaftesbury, had shelters built where the cabbies could revive themselves with a cheap meal and a drink—nonalcoholic, of course. As these shelters were on the public highway, none was allowed to be larger than a horse and cart. They nonetheless managed to accommodate a working kitchen and around ten diners. A handful of these much-loved tongue-and-groove wooden shelters, painted a distinctive dark green, remain—all are now "Grade II listed buildings."

PLATE 9

BROMPTON ROAD ON A FOGGY EVENING

In the early years of the twentieth century, Brompton Road was London's prime fashionable shopping center.

Harrods had started in 1834 in the East End as a wholesale grocery store with a special tea section but, in 1849, Charles Harrod moved the business to the far more profitable Knightsbridge. The Great Exhibition of 1851 was a boon for the founder, and business took off. However, over the years, fires took their toll; more land was acquired and the decision was made to rebuild. The new Harrods store, constructed between 1901 and 1905, dominated the skyline toward the east end of Brompton Road. A palatial terra-cotta emporium with lavish Art Nouveau decoration, Harrods more than fulfilled its ambition to sell "Everything for Everybody Everywhere." "Everything" included houses, yachts, and even funerals. Shoppers were already accustomed to the store's audacious style after the world's first escalator was installed in the previous store (on the same site) in 1898.

Harrods was also one of the first stores to extend credit to its customers, but they were the likes of Oscar Wilde, Ellen Terry, and Lilly Langtry.

Harrods' neighbors included the luxury retailer Harvey Nichols, plus countless smaller shops, all serving the capital's prosperous upper and middle classes. Business was boosted by the opening of the Piccadilly Line tube (subway) in 1906; Brompton Road had its own station, which was closed in 1934 when the entrance to the Knightsbridge station was moved closer to Harrods.

Should shopping pall, the treasures of the Victoria and Albert Museum were nearby. In 1909, these were moved into the museum's ornate and costly new building, opened by King Edward VII.

PLATE 10

OXFORD STREET FROM THE CORNER OF BOND STREET

Since the earliest of times, Oxford Street has democratically catered to shoppers—rich, not so rich, and poor—whereas Bond Street has always provided luxury goods and fine jewelry for the überwealthy.

As late as 1700, the naturalist and writer Thomas Pennant described Oxford Street as "a deep hollow road, and full of sloughs; with here and there a ragged house, the lurking place of cut throats." Then came development: the Pantheon, described as "an enchanted palace" where concerts, exhibitions, and masked balls took place; the apothecary, who sold de Quincey opium; and the Princess's Theatre, named in honor of Queen Victoria.

By the end of the nineteenth century, chameleon-like Oxford Street had changed again and was now dominated by small shops—cloth dealers, fruit vendors, and shoemakers. These, in turn, gave way to department stores such as Selfridges, which opened in 1909 and which still dominates the street today, jostling with street merchants selling discount goods and fruit.

If Oxford Street merchants served the masses, those on Bond Street sorted out the stylish and extremely wealthy and were prepared to cater to any whim. The daintily luxurious Dogs' Toilet Club allowed ladies of fashion to deposit their dogs while they shopped till they dropped. The canines were shampooed in tin baths by dedicated manservants in shirt sleeves and braces, dried, brushed, combed, and then fed with tidbits. On her return, their mistress would pick out a new canine costume—a favorite of 1896 being the "Lonsdale," a fetching made-to-measure driving coat in fawn cloth lined with dark red silk, a cape of the same, and an adorable frill around the neck. The whole was finished off with two gold bells and a fur collar edging to match that of their human companion.

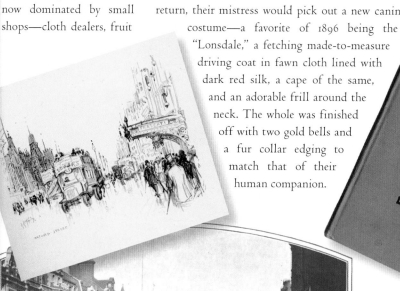

PLATE 11

A PINCH OF SALT

Rose Barton's view of children was refreshingly straightforward; to her, they were not the sugary image of the middle classes.

Pigeons were part of London life, more accepted in Rose Barton's day than in modern London. Feeding them was something everyone did: from the workmen eating lunch in St. Paul's churchyard to the small girl in this picture. Rose Barton clearly had an affection for children, which was lucky, as they invariably plagued her from the moment she set up her easel and took out her paints. Sketching in Hyde Park one day, she noticed a small boy climbing up a tree to rob a wood pigeon's nest of the eggs. The only way to stop him was bribery, so she offered him sixpence if he took only two eggs. He duly took the two eggs, climbed down, accepted the sixpence, and walked away, laughing, with his friends. "I thought there seemed to be a good deal of tittering among the boys as they walked away," she wrote,

"but it was not for some time afterwards that it was explained to me that there are never more than two eggs in a pigeon's nest."

Rose Barton used London children as models, finding them willing subjects. Her sitters were working-class, looked after by their elder sisters, who after the age of seven were rarely seen with a doll, turning into nursemaids instead. Once set up, she was invariably surrounded by young critics. "A small boy once stood (I should think for quite an hour) watching me intently—as I thought, in silent admiration. Up comes a pal, with the familiar 'That's all roight—aint it?' 'I don't know,' said my critic: 'it looks better than it did; but you wouldn't have thought much of it if you'd a seen it 'alf an hour ago.'"

PLATE 12

SPRING-TIME

Rose Barton's picture of two very small children looking intently at the daffodils in a London park
is a perfect nineteenth-century image, conjuring up the illustrated literature of the time.

The golden age of children's writing was a rich vein that artists could draw on, taking in the likes of Christina Rossetti's *Sing-Song: A Nursery Rhyme Book* of 1872, and Charles Kingsley's 1862 *Water Babies*.

It was Lewis Carroll's *Alice's Adventures in Wonderland*, published in 1865, that had the most profound impact. Children's stories and poetry now dealt with fantastic adventures; they were full of strange characters and happenings, taking hold of the imagination in a totally new way. Just as importantly, children's book illustration as an art form was ushered in with Sir John Tenniel's drawings for the Alice books. But it was Kate Greenaway whose pictures came to sum up the carefree lives of Victorian children. Her first book of verse, *Under the Window*, published in 1879, showed children in idyllic settings, surrounded by flowers and birds. In the 1880s and 1890s, only two others rivaled her in popularity.

Walter Crane (1845–1915), an influential member of the arts and crafts movement, began illustrating nursery rhymes in 1864 and became famous for his pictures in *The Frog Prince* and the wonderful 1882 edition of *Household Stories from Grimm*. The first Christmas books produced by Randolph Caldecott (1846–86) in 1878 were such a success that he produced two more each year until he died. *Peter Pan* by J. M. Barrie, published in 1902, Kenneth Grahame's *The Wind in the Willows* (1908), and Frances Hodgson Burnett's *The Secret Garden* (1911) all became classics of children's storytelling, and are still popular today.

The depiction of the perfect world of Edwardian fantasy continued with A. A. Milne's Winnie-the-Pooh books, published in the 1920s, though by then the innocence of the former age had been swept away in the horrors of World War I.

PLATE 13

ISTHMIAN CLUB, PICCADILLY

The streets around Piccadilly and St. James's, a brief stroll from Green Park, were home to Edwardian London's clubs.

The Edwardian period in London was the great age of the gentlemen's club, where, for an annual fee of ten guineas, one could get a cheap dinner, smoke in the library, doze in an armchair, or even live—tended by trained valets who would dress and shave the members, and guarded by doormen to keep out unwanted guests.

The Reform Club (for civil servants), the Carlton (for Conservatives), and the Athenaeum (for bishops) boasted some of the most distinctive buildings in London, and dominated the landscape around Pall Mall. Clubs like Boodle's and White's on St. James's Street, where the richest playboys gambled the night away with the Prince of Wales before he

became Edward VII—or more exotic ones like the Oriental or Travellers—allowed the upper middle classes to behave like bachelors and therefore attracted the implacable opposition of the women's magazines. There were also the junior branches, like the Junior United Service, or those that specialized in sports, like the Turf. All had their own style, grand staircases, brass door handles, and comfortable chairs. This was the era when the humorist P. G. Wodehouse was young, and something of the atmosphere of the Edwardian club scene can be gleaned from his fictional clubs, like the notorious Junior Ganymede for gentlemen's valets.

The Isthmian Club, at 105 Piccadilly, occupied the buildings once known as Hertford House, built in the Italian style in 1850 to house the prodigious art collection of the fourth Marquis of Hertford, which eventually formed the basis of the Wallace Collection in Manchester Square. The Isthmian opened in 1882, restricted to members who had been to a British "public school" or university, and advertised itself as particularly suited for those interested in cricket and rowing.

PLATE 14

SAILING-BOATS ON THE SERPENTINE

The Serpentine was created when Queen Caroline, wife of George II, embarked on a landscaping project in Kensington Gardens to provide a majestic backdrop for Kensington Palace.

The Serpentine—the part in Kensington Gardens is known as the Long Water—was formed when eleven natural ponds in the river Westbourne, which runs through the park en route to the Thames, were dammed by order of Queen Caroline, wife of George II, in 1730. Boating was introduced in 1847, and ice-skating and fishing were also allowed. Initially, boating was not always an idyllic experience—the Westbourne was regularly contaminated with sewage, and a thick layer of putrid mud accumulated. In the late 1860s, the problem was resolved by piping the river and supplying the lake with storm water and surface drainage.

Until the 1930s, only men and boys were allowed in the water, and then only before 8:00 a.m. and after 7:30 p.m. This was one of the few opportunities ordinary folk had to enjoy Hyde Park's facilities, and *Baedeker* describes a crowd of men and boys, "most of them in very homely attire . . . undressing and plunging into the water, where their lusty shouts and hearty laughter testify to their enjoyment." Both sexes were allowed to swim at all hours when the "Serpentine Lido" opened in 1931. The Serpentine Swimming Club, founded in 1864, is still going strong—members swim every day from 6:30 to 9:30 a.m., and stage a legendary 100-yard race every Christmas Day, when the water temperature is usually below 39 degrees Fahrenheit.

PLATE 15

THE CROSSING, HYDE PARK CORNER

Hyde Park corner was always an important and busy junction, originally the site of a
tollgate that marked the entrance to London from the west.

This magnificent stone screen, erected in 1826–29, was designed by Decimus Burton as a formal entrance to Hyde Park, part of a grand scheme that came into being when Buckingham Palace was built in the 1820s. To the right of the screen, Aspley House, home to the Duke of Wellington, was known as No. 1 London, since it was the first house east of the tollgate. The screen's Greek columns contrast with the Roman style of the other great architectural set piece at Hyde Park corner, Constitution Arch (or Wellington Arch, as it is more familiarly known). Also by Decimus Burton, it commemorates the victory at Waterloo in 1815. A statue of the duke originally topped Wellington Arch but was moved to Aldershot (home of the British Army) in 1883. The present statue—*Peace Descending on the Quadriga of War*—replaced it in 1912. Wellington Arch itself was moved to its present position in 1883.

In its heyday in the 1820s and 1830s, Park Lane was home to some of England's grandest families. The imposing mansions they occupied have mostly vanished, many after World War I when the aristocracy was forced to sell its property, and have been replaced by hotels and anonymous blocks of apartments and offices.

In the mid-nineteenth century, when popular radicalism was in favor in London, the Park Lane side of Hyde Park was the scene of many demonstrations. In July 1866, a huge protest took place in favor of the second Reform Bill, which extended the right to vote to many people (but still only to men). Refused permission for a mass rally in the park, the demonstrators tore down the iron railings along Park Lane and surged into the park.

PLATE 16

HYDE PARK CORNER: WET DAY

A quieter scene than usual at Hyde Park corner, which was a spot renowned for traffic congestion by the late nineteenth century.

The building on the left is St. George's Hospital, which was founded in 1733 as an offshoot of Westminster Hospital. The hospital governors rented (initially for £60 per year) Lanesborough House—an ideal location, in their view, on the edge of the city and close to the fresh air of Hyde Park. The buildings became inadequate and, in 1844, were replaced by a fine neo-Greek building designed by William Wilkins; the giant central portico boasts four massive square pillars.

The hospital, which concentrated on acute-care patients, thrived throughout the nineteenth and early twentieth centuries, but lack of space on the site hampered its expansion. Those on the road to recovery were transferred to the Atkinson Morley Convalescent Home in Wimbledon, which was opened by St. George's in 1869 using a £150,000 donation from Atkinson Morley, a wealthy hotel owner who was one of the hospital governors.

The proper training and care of nurses was a priority during most of the nineteenth century. In 1868, the governors resolved to appoint a superintendent to take charge of "the performance of nurses and their moral conduct." The successful candidate was required to be "Church of England, widowed or unmarried, between 30 and 40 years, and to have practical experience and knowledge of nursing."

In 1950, the decision was made to move St. George's to Tooting in southwest London, though it was another thirty years before the move was complete. Now much restored, the old hospital buildings have been converted into a luxury hotel, aptly named the Lanesborough.

PLATE 17

AZALEAS IN BLOOM, ROTTEN ROW

Azaleas and rhododendrons became a staple of Victorian parks and gardens from the mid-nineteenth century onward,
following a series of plant-hunting expeditions in North America and Asia.

In a chapter entitled "Some Places of Fashionable Outdoor Resort," the 1891 edition of *London of To-Day* recommends that visitors seat themselves in one of the chairs along Rotten Row. Here "one may catch a glimpse of the most notable people in London: now of a Cabinet minister; now of a famous ambassador or foreign prince; now of a popular bishop; now of a leading Radical M.P.; now of the Prince of Wales [later King Edward VII] and his sons; now of a City magnate and the ruler of the financial world; now of some famous artist, actor, or popular author . . . For aught one can discern in Rotten Row on a Midsummer morning, all the world is prosperous, dignified,

well-tailored and well-groomed. There is no such thing as poverty, and no such thing as work."

There was another side to London life far removed from the fashionable West End. Just two years earlier, Charles Booth had published the results of his pioneering survey in *Life and Labour of the People in London*. He classified 30 percent of the population of the County of London as either "very poor" (that is, "at all times more or less 'in want' ") or "poor," and wrote that "their lives are an unending struggle, and lack comfort." There was little or no help or support for these people—fewer than 3 percent of Londoners received welfare.

PLATE 18

IN KENSINGTON GARDENS

The beauty of Kensington Gardens has refreshed and inspired the weary citizens of London for more than 200 years.

In 1689, William III, who suffered from asthma and was looking for a tranquil home, bought Nottingham House to convert into Kensington Palace, along with what was originally part of Hyde Park. His wife, Queen Mary, had the gardens laid out with low yew and box hedges in the formal Dutch style. These were promptly uprooted by Queen Anne, who "transferred" a further thirty acres of Hyde Park to her home and, in 1704, created the Orangery. However, it was Queen Caroline, the wife of George II (1727–60), who molded the Kensington Gardens into the beautiful form they now possess, using water from the Westbourne stream to create the Serpentine and the Long Water. George II opened the gardens to the "respectably dressed"—on Saturdays only—but it was not until the reign of William IV (1830–37) that they were opened to the public all year round.

In 1880, the Duke of Cambridge's dog was run over outside Victoria Lodge; it was buried in the small garden behind. Now rather neglected, it was once a well-kept pet cemetery, and headstones commemorating the lives of much-adored monkeys, dogs, and cats can still be seen.

Although Kensington Gardens is laid out formally, it still attracts a wealth of bird life—178 species have so far been identified—while the Round Pond is home to three-spined sticklebacks, roach, gudgeon, and eels.

The beauty of Kensington Gardens has inspired myriad artists and writers, including J. M. Barrie, who strolled there a hundred years ago entertaining the children of his friend Sylvia Llewellyn Davies with fanciful, magical tales—from which sprung *Peter Pan*. A bronze statue of this eternal child, its pedestal covered with squirrels, rabbits and mice, is a perennial favorite in the gardens with children and adults alike. The film *Finding Neverland*, Barrie's biography, was shot here in 2004.

PLATE 19

BY THE RING, HYDE PARK: EVENING

Britain's reputation as a nation of dog lovers took root in the nineteenth century.

On an autumn evening, a fashionably dressed young woman takes her dog for a walk in Hyde Park. The sight was a familiar one—keeping pets, particularly dogs, was as popular for all classes in Victorian and Edwardian times as it is today. Dog collar sellers thronged the streets, dog troughs were built beside drinking fountains, specialty grooming salons looked after the beauty side, and dogs regularly performed in theaters. Battersea Dogs' Home was started in Holloway in 1860 and moved to Battersea in 1871. Dogs were even put to use collecting for charity, with collection boxes strapped to their backs. Their work was acknowledged on dog collars inscribed with the likes of "Presented to Wimbledon Jack by the Parade Committee for his work in the Cause of Charity."

And then there was Charles Cruft, born in Bloomsbury in 1846. Cruft worked for James Spratt, the first dog biscuit manufacturer, and traveled to dog shows in Britain and Europe. Spotting a niche in the market, he launched the First Great Terrier Show in 1886 with fifty-seven classes and 600 entries. But it was not until 1891 that the first Cruft's Greatest Dog Show was launched at the Royal Agricultural Hall in Islington. All breeds were invited to compete, and the show attracted around 2,000 canines. By the end of the century, entries had risen to more than 3,000, with dogs coming from as far away as Russia. Dog mania had arrived. Dog funerals could be ornate, complete with hymns and poems. Then one could either have one's pet stuffed, to sit forever in the parlor, or purchase a decent burial plot, such as in the dogs' cemetery in Kensington Gardens, where all kinds of animals, including monkeys, found their final resting place.

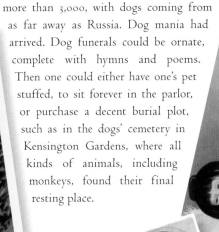

Plate 20

WAITING FOR ROYALTY

"Early in 1901 the Metropolis heard with great satisfaction that King Edward and
Queen Alexandra intended to spend far more time in the Capital than Queen Victoria did."

Mrs. Belloc-Lowndes' pronouncement in *Living London* in 1902, a year after the death of Queen Victoria, would have been greeted enthusiastically by the general public. Scenes such as Rose Barton's decorous crowd waiting for the royal family to appear were likely to become more frequent, for the sight of the royal family has always had a wide appeal. After the death of Prince Albert, Queen Victoria had become a recluse and her court was rigidly and tightly controlled; the new king and queen, on the other hand, were far more relaxed. On a fine spring or summer's day, Queen Alexandra and one of her daughters would drive around Hyde Park in an open carriage. Traffic stopped, hats were lifted, bows made. She was also frequently seen at exhibitions, at church, or visiting friends and relatives, though on these occasions she would choose a relatively modest carriage that might not be recognized. The grand set pieces of the royal family were as formal and colorful as any onlooker could want, particularly when a wealthy "continental royal" was passing through.

It was not only the crowds who loved such occasions; London's well-known jewelry and art dealers, leather makers, and tailors might net up to £10,000 a week from a Serene or Imperial Highness on a shopping spree. It was the new medium of photography that made the royal family and their numerous uncles, aunts, and cousins—first, second, removed, or otherwise—instantly recognizable. Set portraits were valuable commercial assets, with illustrated papers producing a stream of pictures. Anonymity became more difficult and anyone could spot royal relatives such as Edward and Alexandra's eldest daughter and her husband, the Duke and Duchess of Fife, who lived in a modest mansion in Portman Square; or Edward's younger sister Princess Louise, married to the Duke of Argyll, who lived in Kensington Palace.

GALA PERFORMANCE at
COVENT GARDEN OPERA HOUSE

PLATE 21

H.R.H. PRINCE GEORGE OF WALES

Fashion dictated that even princes had to follow the custom of dressing in petticoats and skirts when they were young children.

Rose Barton's picture is of young Prince George Edward, who was two years old when this was painted. The fifth child of George V, he became Duke of Kent and married Marina of Greece. Their children (the second Duke of Kent, Princess Alexandra, and Prince Michael of Kent) and their grandchildren play an important part in the current royal family. But George's earlier life was turbulent. When the duke's elder brother Edward VIII abdicated, there was a possibility that George, fourth in line to the throne, could have succeeded him as monarch, as there was no set convention for such a tumultuous act. Constitutionally, any member of the royal family could have become king. But it was

his elder brother, the Duke of York, Edward Albert Christian George Andrew Patrick David, familiarly known as Bertie, who succeeded as George VI. A shy, ill, and genuinely nervous child with a stammer (which was never entirely eradicated), Albert never expected to have the duties of a sovereign thrust upon him. Reluctant as he was to become king, he served his country with dignity and true devotion to duty, even refusing along with his wife, Queen Elizabeth, to leave London during the Blitz of World War II. He took the name George in tribute to his father, and was the father of the British Isles' current monarch, Elizabeth II. He died of lung cancer in 1952.

PRINCE EDWARD OF YORK.

PLATE 22

IN THE STRAND:
WAITING FOR ELECTION NEWS

Home rule for Ireland was the issue of the moment, and it was Gladstone's advocacy of Irish rights
that led to the gradual decline of the Liberal Party.

The *Graphic*, forerunner to the *Daily Graphic*, was founded in December 1869 by William Luson Thomas, a wood engraver who realized the power of the visual in influencing public opinion. Thomas chose some of the most talented artists of his generation to illustrate his new journal, among them John Millais, who cofounded the Pre-Raphaelite Brotherhood with Holman Hunt and Dante Gabriel Rossetti. Thomas first produced the *Graphic* in a modest rented house, but by 1882, he employed 1,000 people and his Christmas edition sold over 500,000 copies. In 1889, the *Graphic* went daily and, on November 4, 1891, it published the first halftone picture in a newspaper, that of George Lambert, a Liberal parliamentary candidate.

The excited crowd gathered outside the offices of the *Daily Graphic* was waiting to hear the results of the 1892 general election. As always, the newspaper ingeniously exhibited cartoons of the two protagonists mounting separate ladders, the rungs below them representing the seats each had won. A burning issue of the day was home rule for Ireland, which was championed by the Liberal leader, William Gladstone. His recognition of Irish demands had wrecked his third ministry in 1886, with many anti–home rule Liberals allying themselves with Lord Salisbury and the Conservatives. Although the Conservatives won the most seats, Gladstone, in coalition with the Irish Nationalists, became the prime minister. He retired in 1894 after the 1893 defeat of his home rule bill in the House of Lords.

PLATE 23

THE ROYAL EXCHANGE

Until the Royal Exchange was built in 1570, international merchants wandered up and down
Lombard Street, negotiating in rain, snow, and sun alike.

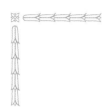

In the early sixteenth century, London was a vibrant center of commerce. On Lombard Street, the center of London banking, European merchants traded and negotiated in taverns, in homes, and in the open air, with all the attendant unpleasant vagaries of the English climate. London, unlike the more sophisticated city of Antwerp, lacked a stock exchange. Richard Gresham, a visionary merchant who supplied King Henry VIII with tapestries for Hampton Court, lobbied actively for a London exchange. However, it was not until 1566 that his son, Thomas, realized his dream, and built an exchange with his own money on land purchased by the City of London. It stood at the junction of Threadneedle Street

and Cornhill. This first Royal Exchange burned to the ground in the Great Fire of 1666. It was rebuilt in 1669—Samuel Pepys witnessed the laying of the foundation stone—and in 1697, Jews were finally admitted as brokers. It was not only goods that were traded here. On May 12, 1766, one John Crouch and his wife were convicted of "offering to sell, on the Royal Exchange, a young girl." The exchange again burned to the ground in 1838, and was rebuilt in 1844. Startlingly, the forecourt of the 'Change, as it was now commonly known, was the first place in Britain to boast public conveniences—although these were only for men.

Pip, the hero of Dickens's *Great Expectations*, visited the 'Change and commented, "I saw fluey men sitting there under the bills about shipping, whom I took to be great merchants, though I couldn't understand why they should all be out of spirits."

It is this building, designed by Sir William Tite, that looms through the dismal gloom of Rose Barton's picture. The Exchange is now a luxury shopping mall.

D. 42486. LONDON: EXCHANGE & BANK.

The Royal Exchange. London.

PLATE 24

CLOTH ALLEY, SMITHFIELD

In Rose Barton's day, anyone who wanted a glimpse of London as it had once been could venture to the last vestiges of the medieval city around Cloth Alley, in the enclave of Cloth Fair in Smithfield.

By 1904, Smithfield was established as London's major meat market, echoing to the early morning sounds of the traffic, the cries of salesmen, and the thump of meat cleavers. But it had traditionally been much more than that: it was London's racecourse, tournament ground, and execution site. This was where the young King Richard II faced down Wat Tyler during the Peasants' Revolt in 1381, and it was where 277 people were burned at the stake for heresy in the reign of Mary Tudor. Even in Rose Barton's day, a large gas lamp commemorated these events. It was also the place where, according to one of Henry VIII's laws, poisoners were boiled to death, and the site where all of medieval London streamed for the notorious Bartholomew Fair—immortalized in Ben Jonson's play of the same name—which was abolished only in 1853.

All that then remained of that great past was Cloth Fair, the few medieval streets behind the church of St. Bartholomew-the-Great. According to the travel writer Augustus Hare, in 1870 it was filled with "old though squalid houses of Elizabethan and Jacobin date."

When Rose Barton was painting, much of the area had been condemned as slums and was being demolished, but the last vestiges of the ancient cloth trade, which had dominated Bartholomew Fair, still clung on. The old hawkers and junk dealers gathered around the Dick Whittington pub, which claimed—quite wrongly—to be the oldest in London.

In 1905, shortly after this painting was finished, the old west gateway to the Cloth Fair was pulled down by the London County Council as part of its plan to clear the slums.

PLATE 25

FLOWER GIRLS IN THE STRAND

In the early 1900s, London's streets still thronged with every variety of street vendor crying their wares with distinctive singsong phrases of the likes sung by Rose Barton's flower sellers: "Buy my flowers, two bunches a penny!"

Besides the essentials of life—fruit, vegetables, meat, and fish—the street merchants sold curds and whey, Dutch biscuits (gingerbread), old clothes, combs, and ink for the professional classes. Street craftsmen ground scissors, mended chairs, and cobbled. And flower girls were everywhere—although in reality many were elderly matrons, their bodies swathed in long shawls, their heads covered with large, solid hats, often decorated with flowers and feathers. The little fountain in Rose Barton's picture stood until the early 1900s in front of St. Mary le Strand, marking the place where the first hackney coach stand was set up in 1634.

The flower girls flocked to Covent Garden market in the early morning, where they bought the fresh flowers that filled the open straw baskets hanging from their necks. Many young, poor girls—orphaned, forsaken, abused—sold flowers in the market itself. At the end of the day, they would gather up the unsold, wilting flowers and turn them into little nosegays, which they hawked to the wealthy on their way to the Royal Opera House. In 1974, the fruit and vegetable market moved to Battersea, and Covent Garden was restored. It is now a vibrant, thriving area with shops, street performers, and a craft market. To celebrate its silver anniversary, six statues were commissioned, one of which is the most glamorous, gorgeous, vivacious flower girl of all, the fictional Eliza Doolittle, heroine of George Bernard Shaw's *Pygmalion*, which was turned into the film *My Fair Lady*.

LONDON TYPES: A FLOWER SELLER.

PLATE 26

RUS IN URBE

This little red-roofed cottage stood at the corner of Glebe Place, King's Road, Chelsea. A generation before Rose Barton, the artist Cecil Lawson painted the gardens near Glebe Place and called it *Rus in Urbe*—"the country in the city."

In the Edwardian era as it is now, the rise and fall of the fortunes of different neighborhoods in London was the topic of dinner party conversation in the city. Although the streets near the river at Chelsea had been occupied by artists like Whistler or writers like Wilde at the end of the Victorian period, other parts of the neighborhood were now becoming respectable too. An Act of Parliament was passed in 1870 to lease the so-called Glebe lands, which had been market gardens belonging to the local

church, and the area was quickly developed. Houses were built on streets like Bramerton Street and Glebe Place and new shops on the King's Road, the street that would become such a magnet for fashionable shoppers decades later. Glebe Place itself was built on the site of an old pottery workshop run by the Wedgwood company and an old Huguenot chapel. One cottage on the street was reputed to have been Henry VIII's hunting lodge.

When Rose Barton was painting, this part of Chelsea still had a literary feel about it. Had not George Meredith and Algernon Charles Swinburne chosen to live nearby? But now the new garden studios in Glebe Place were attracting London's artistic elite. The artist George Boyce lived there until his death in 1896 and commissioned a new house from the Victorian architect Philip Webb. The sculptor Giovanni Fontana lived nearby, and soon Glebe Place proved to be a magnet, pulling other artists into the surrounding area. Cecil Lawson had died in 1882, but Rose Barton's tribute to him showed that, despite the development and the new houses, Edwardian residents of Chelsea could still feel a sense of the country within the city.

PLATE 27

OLD RIVER-WALL, CHELSEA

From the earliest of times, the Thames has been the lifeblood of London, stimulating both trade and urban development.

The Thames was especially crucial to Chelsea's development, as it allowed residents to travel easily to London and other riverside settlements. Since around 1300, more prosperous residents had their own wharves and used barges to travel up and down the stream. Watermen were also available for hire—in 1705, it took about an hour to reach London—and these men continued to ply their trade well into the nineteenth century. In 1816, a steamboat service served Chelsea, and by 1844, eight steamboats traveled between London Bridge and Chelsea four times an hour. By 1908, the steam service had been withdrawn, as denizens of Chelsea and elsewhere preferred to travel by the expanding road and rail system.

James Abbott McNeill Whistler (1834–1903) lived and painted in Chelsea until 1879, when he went bankrupt and was forced to sell his house. Luckily, he still had sufficient funds to cheer himself up with a visit to Venice, where he worked on a set of etchings. One of Whistler's most beautiful works is *Nocturne: Blue and Silver—Chelsea 1871*, a tranquil view of Chelsea and the Thames from Battersea Bridge. The painting now hangs in the Tate Britain.

PLATE 28

THE LAST LAMP, THAMES EMBANKMENT

"The winter evening settles down
With smells of steaks in passageways . . .
And at the corner of the street
A lonely cab-horse steams and stamps.
And then the lighting of the lamps."

The lines from T. S. Eliot's poem "Preludes" and Rose Barton's picture evoke a romantic ideal. In the nineteenth and early twentieth centuries, lamplighters were a familiar sight, making their way slowly along the rows of gaslights, illuminating them one by one.

Gas lights were introduced at the beginning of the nineteenth century in London, amazing visitors who knew nothing except dark streets or roads dimly lit by oil lamps. With the safety of citizens a serious issue, and the huge profits waiting to be made by private suppliers, gaslights spread rapidly, and by 1823, 213 streets in London were lit by 40,000 streetlamps. In the 1840s, Oxford Street and Tottenham Court Road had four different companies supplying gas from five different stations, and in the same decade, Buckingham Palace and the new Houses of Parliament installed gas lamps. By now, most of London's main streets were gaslit except for Grosvenor Square, whose residents considered it vulgar.

The invention of the gas mantle by a chemist at Bunsen's laboratory in Heidelberg in 1886 revolutionized gas lighting, although initially the mantles were expensive, inefficient, and fragile. Improvements followed fast, and the new mantles were used in street lighting in London for the first time in 1895. By now, electricity was a viable alternative, with the Gaiety Theatre, London Bridge Station, and the offices of the *Times* leading the way with electric lights in the 1870s. Electricity slowly replaced gas, and in 1933, still only half of London's streets were lit by electricity. Although the method of lighting changed, the old fittings were kept and adapted, and some of the elegant former gas lamps can still be seen along the Embankment.

PLATE 29

WHO IS IT?

Looking like an Old Testament prophet in a dressing gown, the statue of Thomas Carlyle, the great historian and philosopher, stood in Rose Barton's day—as it does now—by the river Thames in Chelsea.

Carlyle, an intellectual giant and the prophet of the Victorian age, died in 1881. By the time Rose Barton painted the statue with the pile of books cast at Carlyle's feet, he had been dead for a quarter of a century. But there were those living near the Chelsea Embankment, where the statue stood, who remembered him wandering down the King's Road with his dog Nero, or riding in the open fields across the river that had since become Battersea Park.

For nearly fifty years he had lived nearby, in a house at 5 Cheyne Row (later No. 24), fighting long battles with his neighbors, their noisy parrot, and their daughter's piano lessons, which drove the great writer to distraction. In fact, Carlyle and his wife Jane lived a difficult life. Jane's health was broken by his constant demands and nervous hammering on the wall with a poker and by her addiction to sleep aids, and she died in 1866 of heart failure as she rode in a carriage around Hyde Park. Carlyle's books on the French Revolution and Oliver Cromwell, and his championing of the idea of the hero in politics and history, made him famous, and the writers

and revolutionaries of the age beat a path to his door.

He hated artists, but made an exception for sculptor Joseph Boehm, who had been a historical researcher for him. But he warned him at the start of the first sitting that resulted in this statue: "I'll give you twenty-two minutes to see what you can do with me." In fact, he stayed the course, and this was the result.

Carlyle's house at Cheyne Row was made into a museum after his death.

24 CHEYNE ROW.
CHELSEA.

PLATE 30

ENTRANCE TO THE APOTHECARIES' GARDEN

For three and a half centuries, the Apothecaries' Garden, now known as the Chelsea Physic Garden, has gathered plants
from all over the world in order to research their healing properties and to conserve them for the future.

The Chelsea Physic Garden was, for hundreds of years, a secret paradise, a mystical, wondrous place that could only be glimpsed longingly through its huge, wrought-iron gates; a magical yet forbidding world of exotic plants, both beautiful and possessing potent powers. It was founded in 1673 so that members of the Worshipful Society of Apothecaries might learn to recognize the herbs and flowers so important to their calling. In 1671, the society had established an "Elaboratory" at its hall in Cobham House, Blackfriars—the first "factory" to produce drugs on a large scale.

Chelsea was chosen for the garden's location, as the Thames creates its own warm microclimate that allows plants from more forgiving climes to survive icy British winters; the Physic Garden boasts the largest fruiting olive tree in Britain.

In contemporary times, the garden plays a major role in public education, focusing on the West's resurgence of interest in natural medicines. It continues to research the properties, origins, and conservation of more than 5,000 species. It is also home to the Garden of World Medicine, Britain's first center for ethnobotany—the study of the botany of different ethnic groups and indigenous peoples.

Since 1983, the wrought-iron gates have been open to the public from noon to 6:00 p.m. on Sundays and from noon to 5:00 p.m. on Wednesdays from April to October.

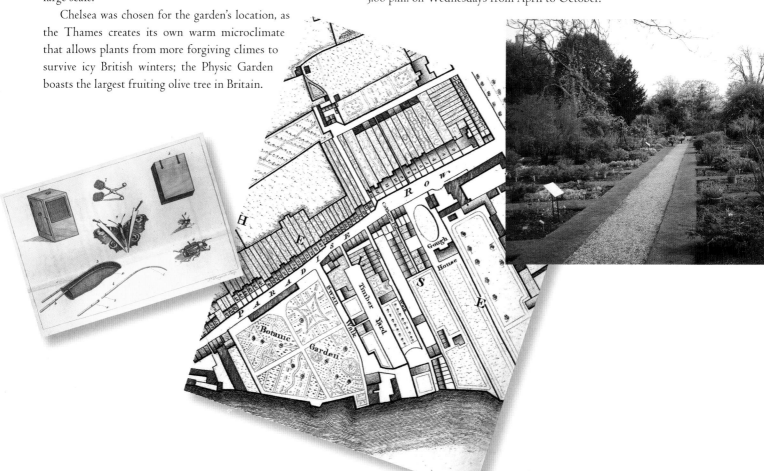

PLATE 31

OUT FOR THE DAY

By 1904, the creation of Battersea Park and the provision of public housing had changed Battersea from an unsavory area into a respectable, lower-middle-class suburb.

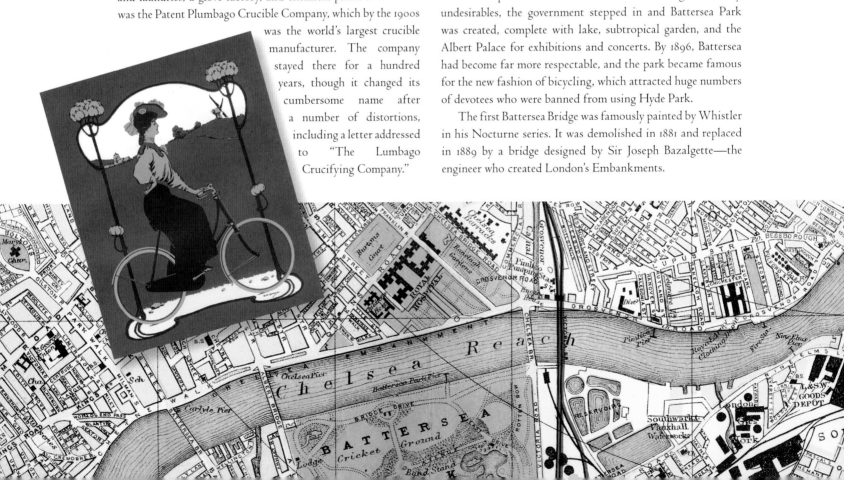

Battersea's long history starts with the Saxons; by Rose Barton's time, the suburb—conveniently just south of the river—had become an important industrial area, boosted by the opening of the London and Southampton Railway in 1838 and its terminus at Nine Elms. The large railway depot and repair works attracted industries large and small—Price's Candle Factory, which also made cycle lamp oil; Orlando Jones' Starch Factory; the Nine Elms Gas Works; and laundries, a glove factory, and chemical plant. Preeminent was the Patent Plumbago Crucible Company, which by the 1900s was the world's largest crucible manufacturer. The company stayed there for a hundred years, though it changed its cumbersome name after a number of distortions, including a letter addressed to "The Lumbago Crucifying Company."

Battersea's population increased significantly to service the growing industries: from just over 3,000 in 1801 to nearly 169,000 by 1901, with public housing like the 1870s Shaftesbury Park Estate replacing the squalid slums of old. During the early nineteenth century, unsalubrious, marshy Battersea Fields was infamous for an 1829 duel between the Duke of Wellington and the Earl of Winchelsea, and for the sport of pigeon shooting on an enclosure called the Subscription Ground. As it was attracting too many undesirables, the government stepped in and Battersea Park was created, complete with lake, subtropical garden, and the Albert Palace for exhibitions and concerts. By 1896, Battersea had become far more respectable, and the park became famous for the new fashion of bicycling, which attracted huge numbers of devotees who were banned from using Hyde Park.

The first Battersea Bridge was famously painted by Whistler in his Nocturne series. It was demolished in 1881 and replaced in 1889 by a bridge designed by Sir Joseph Bazalgette—the engineer who created London's Embankments.

PLATE 32

THE PENSIONERS' GARDEN, ROYAL HOSPITAL, CHELSEA

Old soldiers find a congenial home at the Royal Hospital—their loyal service rewarded with food, clothing, a small allowance, and nursing should they fall ill.

Chelsea pensioners are still a familiar sight on the streets of today's oh-so-fashionable King's Road. Usually they are sporting day wear—navy-blue uniforms—but sometimes they can be glimpsed wearing their scarlet ceremonial dress topped with a three-cornered hat.

Until the seventeenth century, ill and old soldiers were left to fend for themselves. Finally, in 1645, Parliament decreed that the disabled should receive pensions from national funds. But many were still commandeered into garrison duty—terrible for them, and a hindrance to the army. King Charles II, restored to the throne in 1660 after a long civil war and appreciating the loyalty of his men, issued a royal warrant authorizing the building of the

Royal Hospital, Chelsea. By 1692, 476 pensioners were in residence and taking advantage of the magnificent formal gardens designed by the architect Sir Christopher Wren. These were swept away when the Chelsea Embankment was constructed (1871–74), but the pensioners still have sixty-six acres of gorgeous grounds. The world-famous Royal Horticultural Society's Chelsea Flower Show has been held here annually since 1913. In memory of their royal benefactor, the pensioners celebrate Founders Day or Oak Apple Day as near as possible to May 29—Charles II's birthday and the date of his restoration to the throne, and also the day commemorating his miraculous escape from Parliamentary forces after the 1651 Battle of Worcester, when he cunningly hid in an oak tree.

PLATE 33

EMANUEL HOSPITAL, WESTMINSTER

By the time Rose Barton published her painting of Emanuel Hospital in Westminster, with its solitary cat and lonely pensioner in the distance, it had been turned to dust and rubble and transformed into the grand Edwardian hotel, St. James's Court.

This painting is a nostalgic tribute to a London that, even as Rose Barton painted it, was fast disappearing. The hospital was, in fact, demolished in the early 1890s after a long and bitter campaign by conservationists, local dignitaries, and churchmen to preserve it. The hospital was a poorhouse, traditionally housing ten men and ten women—all over the age of fifty-six—and had been built in 1688, the year of the Glorious Revolution. But as an ancient city in its own right, Westminster was filled with charitable institutions and Emanuel Hospital merged with four other charities a few decades before this painting was made.

It was a sign of the times. Institutions that were supposed to tackle poverty—the poorhouses that were set up seventy years before this picture, as well as the charities still operating from centuries before—were coming under increasing pressure from cost cutters and reformers alike. There was talk of old-age pensions, and a royal commission on the subject in 1903, though

it was not until the famous Lloyd George People's Budget of 1909 that such a revolution was finally launched. Meanwhile, the old institutions were feeling the strain of public dissatisfaction.

Even so, when the trustees said they wanted to demolish the ancient hospital in 1889, there was an enormous public outcry about the loss of such a beautiful piece of seventeenth-century architecture. The Charity Commission urged them not to do so; the campaigners took the trustees all the way to the high court, but to no avail. Within five years, the old building was gone.

PLATE 34

NELSON'S COLUMN IN A FOG

Burning coal was synonymous with progress and the Industrial Revolution; given a choice between progress
and clean air, the British chose the former until a four-day fog in 1952 was blamed for the deaths of about 4,000 people.

In this painting of Trafalgar Square, the four massive bronze lions guarding Nelson's Column can barely be seen. Mighty symbols of empire and victory, sculpted by Sir Edwin Landseer and cast from metal said to have once constituted fearsome French cannons, they nonetheless slip undefined into one of the heavy fogs that used to regularly blanket London.

Coal discovered in abundance off the northeast coast of Britain was a cheap, soft, bituminous coal used by most Londoners to heat their homes—but sea coal was a very inefficient fuel that produced great clouds of smoke and very little heat.

This smoke, belching by the 1800s from more than a million homes, combined with natural fog to produce a thick, yellowish-green veil that came to be known as "pea soup" in recognition of its thick, viscous quality and color. This London "soup," which lasted for long day after long day, could frequently be fatal, and many died from the bronchitis and other pulmonary problems that it precipitated.

In a unique example of American one-upmanship, Inez Haynes Irwin, writing in *The Californiacs* in 1921, declared California fog to be British fog's superior, describing it as "not distilled from pea soup like the London fogs; moist air-gauzes rather, pearl-touched and glimmering."

PLATE 35

GORDON'S STATUE

General Charles George Gordon was a true Victorian hero, and his statue was one of the public reminders of England's greatness, along with that of Nelson, assorted admirals, and other generals in Trafalgar Square.

In 1887, a statue of General Gordon by the classical sculptor Sir Hamo Thornycroft was unveiled in Trafalgar Square. The soldier, known as "Chinese Gordon" for his involvement in suppressing the Taiping rebellion in 1864, and then "Gordon Pasha" and, finally, "Gordon of Khartoum," was seen as a swashbuckling, full-blooded Victorian hero. His death in 1885 at the siege of Khartoum, Sudan, turned him into a martyred warrior, the blame for failing to relieve the siege laid firmly by the public at the government's door. Every January 26, the anniversary of his death, the faithful laid wreaths on his statue. Gordon's death was romanticized in a popular painting of 1885 by George William Joy, *General Gordon's Last Stand*, and as recently as 1966 in the film *Khartoum*, in which Charlton Heston rather improbably plays the British general. The debunking of the hero began with Lytton Strachey's *Eminent Victorians* (1918) and continued with Anthony Nutting's *Gordon of Khartoum: Martyr and Misfit* (1966), which suggested that Gordon had defied the government's orders and deliberately refused to evacuate Khartoum while it was still possible to do so.

Gordon's statue was moved in 1943 and reerected in the Victoria Embankment Gardens ten years later. Here, the general still stands, holding the Bible in one hand and the cane he always carried tucked under his arm. A religious man, he visited Palestine in 1882–83 and suggested an alternative location for Golgotha, the site of Christ's crucifixion. This site, known as the Garden Tomb or "Gordon's Calvary," is still considered by many to be the most plausible.

PLATE 36

HASTE TO THE WEDDING

St. George's formed part of the great development of Hanover Square, named in honor of George I, Elector of Hanover.

One of the fifty new churches built as a result of the Act of 1711 to provide places of worship for London's fast-growing populace, St. George's quickly became the venue for the most fashionable of weddings. The new parish was huge, taken from part of the parish of St. Martin-in-the-Fields, and covered the area from Regent Street west to the Serpentine and south from Oxford Street to Mayfair, Belgravia, and Pimlico. It was surrounded by countryside; in 1725, the enthusiastic could shoot woodcock in the Conduit Mead and snipe at the west end of Brook Street.

Designed in 1720–25 by John James, one of Sir Christopher Wren's assistants, and costing £10,000, its position in the first of the three great Mayfair squares and its Corinthian portico, never before seen on a London church, guaranteed success from the start. In 1762, James Boswell was far too distracted by the Duchess of Grafton, who "attracted his eyes too much," to listen to the doubtless worthy sermon. The list of those married here reads like a roll call of the rich, the famous, and the infamous. Twenty-six-year-old Emma Hart married Sir William Hamilton here in 1791, followed by the likes of the poet Percy Bysshe Shelley in 1816 (after his first wife drowned herself in the Serpentine), the writer George Eliot (Mary Ann Evans) in 1880 to John Walter Cross, Theodore Roosevelt in 1886 to his childhood sweetheart, and, two years after Rose Barton's picture, the politician Henry Asquith. By this time, however, the church had lost its fashionable edge, and St. Paul's, Knightsbridge, had become the choice for top society weddings.

George Frederick Handel, who lived on nearby Brook Street, was a parishioner from 1724 to 1759, frequently playing on the organ. The church's association with the German composer continues with the annual Handel Festival, where it is the venue for many of the concerts.

PLATE 37

FIRE

"Perhaps there is no more awful sound in the world—especially at night—than the sudden cry of 'Fire!' "

This extract from Rose Barton's text might seem a trifle melodramatic, but fire was one of the worst—and one of the most feared—dangers in Victorian and Edwardian London. In 1834, most of the Palace of Westminster burned down, and a fire at the Tower of London in 1841 destroyed the Grand Armoury and caused £250,000 worth of damage. During the nineteenth century, firefighting equipment and methods improved, but devastating fires continued to take their toll—in November 1897, a hundred buildings were destroyed in Cripplegate at a cost of £1 million.

The huge warehouses along the river were particularly prone to fire; riverside inhabitants regularly capitalized on the disasters—a tea warehouse caught fire, the

boxes were thrown into the river, and the next morning young entrepreneurs appeared with thin cotton bags, scooping up the floating tea, which they then sold.

Firefighters had their heroes, one of the most famous being a dog called Chance, from the Watling Street Fire Station, who ran up ladders into burning buildings to dig in the rubble. If he found anyone, he would run back to his master and bark. Easily identified by his collar, which read "Stop me not but onward let me jog, for I am the London firemen's dog," Chance was stuffed after his death and exhibited at fairgrounds.

Horses continued to pull the fire engines through the streets until 1904, when the Metropolitan Fire Brigade was renamed the London Fire Brigade. In 1914, one-fifth of the London Fire Brigade was in the navy reserve and was called up for service in World War I, leaving the fire service seriously undermanned.

PLATE 38

ST. MARY'S-LE-STRAND

Once a building of great beauty adjacent to land used for happy festivities, by Rose Barton's time
St. Mary le Strand was already becoming eclipsed by noise and traffic.

St. Mary le Strand (as it now known) was one of fifty new churches a 1711 Act of Parliament decreed should be built to provide places of worship for London's rapidly expanding population.

Until the sixteenth century, the Strand was essentially a line of bishops' palaces. These fashionable residences were seized after the Restoration of 1660 and Edward, Lord Protector, set about building for himself in their stead a renaissance palace—Somerset House. As this grandiose project mushroomed, the old church, which dated back to at least 1147, was demolished to provide yet more stone for Edward's monumental project.

The adjoining green had been home to a maypole, a focus for festivities. The Puritans, unsurprisingly, destroyed the maypole in the Strand in 1644, but it was—to the delight of London's children—later replaced on several occasions. The last maypole in the Strand was commandeered by Isaac Newton in 1718 to support the highest telescope in the world, based in Wanstead.

Elegantly built in the Baroque style by the great Scottish architect James Gibb, the present St. Mary le Strand was originally intended to be flanked by a 250-foot-high column topped by a Florentine-executed brass statue of Queen Anne. Fortunately for the beauty of the church, Queen Anne died and the church was instead surmounted by a Christopher Wren–inspired graceful spire.

Sadly, St. Mary le Strand is now marooned on a traffic island.

PLATE 39

DRINKING-FOUNTAIN IN ST. JAMES'S PARK

In the nineteenth century, the only clean water available to the poor of
London was provided by water fountains built by philanthropists.

In the nineteenth century, the Thames was filthy, polluted, and full of untreated sewage. In 1849, as yet another cholera epidemic hit London, one poor, desperate denizen wrote in a letter to the *Times*: "We ain't got no privez, no dustbins, no drains, no water-splies, and no drain or suer in the hole place." Fifty thousand died of cholera that year alone.

Finally, in 1859, the Metropolitan Free Drinking Fountain Association, supported by many eminent citizens, including the Archbishop of Canterbury and Prince Albert, was set up by Samuel Gurney, a member of Parliament. Its first fountain, on the railings of St. Sepulchre-without-Newgate church, was unveiled on April 21, 1859, and was soon being used by more than 7,000 people a day. By 1870, 140 fountains had been created. As man suffered, so did his best friend, the dog, and so the fountains had little dog troughs attached to them. Cattle troughs (153 of them) had also been built to help address the plight of horses—50,000 a day were using them by 1885—and the many thirsty creatures driven to London for the market.

Many of these fountains, such as this St. James's Park Greek Boy Fountain (1863) by Lady von Gleichen, were not only utilitarian; they were, as Rose Barton's painting shows, also beautiful. The original at St. Sepulchre's has been restored and can be seen in all its glory with marble arch, base, and two cups attached.

The association, which was renamed the Metropolitan Drinking Fountain and Cattle Trough Association in 1867, continues to provide water fountains for schools and water wells for developing countries; it is also committed to the restoration of its original "lifesavers."

PLATE 40

FEEDING THE GULLS FROM THE BRIDGE IN ST. JAMES'S PARK

St. James's Park not only provides a place for weary humanity to recharge
its batteries; it is also a valuable urban refuge for wildlife.

St. James's Park was originally a dank, marshy field used by the adjoining leper hospital to graze pigs. The park took its name from the hospital.

Henry VIII, the monarch who first drained the fields, used the land as a skittle alley and nursery for his deer, but it was Charles II (1630–85) who converted a chain of small ponds into the long waterway known as the Canal. Birds and waterfowl abounded, indigenous and exotic: iridescent green-headed mallards, a disabled crane with a wooden leg, and a pair of huge pelicans that were a gift from the Russian ambassador. The pelicans' descendants still live in the park, their antics delighting visitors. Feeding time—fresh fish, naturally—is at 3:00 p.m. Charles II, accompanied by various mistresses, also loved to feed his avian subjects, and sometimes even swam among them, much to the fascination of the ordinary people who thronged the park.

Architect John Nash softened the harsh lines of the Canal and created a more natural-looking lake that was spanned by an ornamental bridge in 1814, a striking confection of yellow, black, and red. The bridge in this painting is the later iron suspension bridge of 1857 designed by James Digby Wyatt. It, too, has since been demolished, but the swooping, calling gulls and bread-loving ducks remain.

PLATE 41

PARLIAMENT STREET

Parliament Street, now the epitome of social respectability, has a colorful past.

Parliament Street, originally a narrow alley linking Charing Cross to Westminster, first appeared on the capital's tax rolls in 1750. Over the years it has undergone tremendous building and rebuilding, so much so that by 1982 only two of the original eighteenth-century houses remained: Nos. 43 and 44. Much of the street has been sensitively restored and rebuilt to provide purpose-built accommodation for Parliament.

It is, however, not the architecture that gives Parliament Street its real claim to fame but the varied and colorful individuals who have inhabited it. Isambard Kingdom Brunel, denizen of No. 53, connected his apartment with that of his friend opposite, Sir George Burke, by a piece of string, much to the bemusement of the other residents of Parliament Street. In fact, there was a bell at Burke's end, which Brunel used to wake Burke in the morning or to call him to the window to "receive his telegraphic communications."

Foremost among Parliament Street's residents must, however, be Maundy Gregory, the "honors broker," or procurer of funds, to the prime minister, Lloyd George. So corrupt was Gregory, the son of a vicar, whose plush offices were at No. 38, that in 1925 legislation was finally passed to make this age-old practice illegal—although this did not prevent former prime minister Tony Blair from becoming embroiled in questions about cash for honors. Maundy moved into "fund-raising" for the Roman Catholic Church and the selling of papal honors before buying a hotel in Dorking, soon to be acclaimed as "the biggest brothel in southeast England," and allegedly turning his hand to murder. His alcoholic girlfriend, Edith Rosse, was undoubtedly poisoned, slipping into paralysis and death days after changing her will in his favor.

Maundy was not the only murderer to wander Parliament Street. Thomas Neill Cream purchased the strychnine he needed to dispatch prostitutes in Lambeth from the apothecary Priest's, at No. 22. However, unlike Maundy, who was never prosecuted, Cream was convicted for his crimes; he was executed by hanging on November 16, 1892.

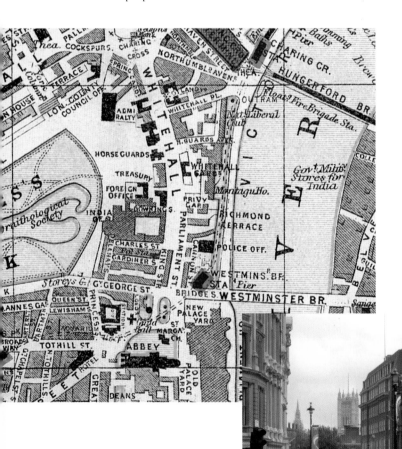

PLATE 42

CHANGING GUARD, WHITEHALL

Great palaces all had tiltyards where fighting men could train and practice their swordplay.
Through what is now the gate to Horse Guards Parade—guarded by the Royal Horse Guards
with their shiny breastplates—one can still glimpse what was once the tiltyard for
Whitehall Palace, where Henry VIII held his greatest tournaments.

Whitehall Palace disappeared in flames in 1698, thanks to the carelessness of a Dutch laundry woman. When Rose Barton was painting, Whitehall—the very heart of the empire—was being transformed from a ramshackle series of Georgian terraces into a mighty engine of government, with new buildings in a confident and solid imperial style. The new War Office building and the new Colonial Office, both emerging from scaffolding at this time, were designed to demonstrate to the world the solidity and strength of the British empire.

Whitehall is the road to the Palace of Westminster, the heart of democracy, and was the scene of the execution of Charles I—outside the Banqueting House and just opposite this spot—in 1649. Only members of the royal family are allowed to drive through the gate to Horse Guards.

There on the parade ground beyond it, in Rose Barton's day, between the pomposity of Whitehall and the calm of St. James's Park, the official guard for King Edward VII changed every day at 11:00 a.m.—or 10:00 a.m. on Sundays—and was relieved every hour until 4:00 p.m.

No matter whether the king himself was relaxing in Monte Carlo, on his yacht at Cowes, or at one of those innumerable country house parties to which the Edwardian aristocracy was addicted, and with the royal standard missing from the roof of Buckingham Palace—the guard still changed. It was as regular as the chimes of Big Ben, and was intended to appear so. The same ritual continues to this day.

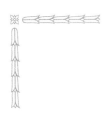

ENTERING THE HORSE GUARDS

PLATE 43

ST. BARTHOLOMEW'S HOSPITAL

St. Bartholomew's Hospital has been treating the sick for almost 900 years.

St. Bartholomew's Hospital, or Bart's as it is usually called, is London's oldest hospital, dating back to the reign of Henry I (1068–1135). One of Henry's courtiers, Rahere, a jester or jongleur, felt the need to visit Rome to atone for his sinful lifestyle. While abroad, mortally ill with malarial fever, he prayed on the island of St. Bartholomew—also home to the temple of Aesculapius, the Greek god of healing—that he might at least live long enough to die in England. St. Bartholomew, as the story goes, appeared, surrounded by light in a wondrous vision, and announced that he had "chosen a place in the suburbs of London at Smoothfield [now Smithfield] where in my name thou shalt found a church and hospital."

Henry I gave Rahere authority for the construction, and building began on the muddy piece of ground that was Smoothfield. St. Bartholomew surely gave his blessing to this great hospital, for since that date, it has unceasingly given succor to the destitute and ill. It was one of only three hospitals to survive Henry VIII's Reformation—the others being St. Thomas's on Lambeth Palace Road and Bethlem (Bedlam) on Lambeth Road, a madhouse where in medieval times the inmates were chained to the wall and, when violent, were whipped or ducked under water. Bedlam moved out of London in 1930 and part of the building became the home of the Imperial War Museum in 1936. Bart's is now a teaching hospital of world-famous repute.

PLATE 44

THE GUARDS MARCHING
NEAR ST. JAMES'S PALACE

The to and fro of groups of guardsmen, in their distinctive red tunics and bearskins,
was—as it is now—one of the most distinctive sights of London.

There were then, as there are today, five regiments of guards—infantry regiments whose duties include guarding the two royal residences, Buckingham Palace and nearby St. James's. Their morning marches, changing guard or simply moving between the barracks and the palace, have always attracted crowds, as Rose Barton shows here, with a distinctive London mixture of bowler hats and prams.

There has been a building at St. James's since before the Norman conquest, when there was a hospital for lepers on the site. Henry VIII pulled this down, enclosed St. James's Park for himself, and built the dark redbrick palace that is the scene for this painting. It was here that a bitter, miserable Queen Mary Tudor eked out her final days, and here that Charles I spent the night before his execution in 1649.

In Edwardian London, St. James's Palace was a peculiar survival, largely destroyed by fire a century before, used occasionally for state banquets, and still officially giving its name—the Court of St. James—to the royal court to which foreign ambassadors were attached. When Rose Barton painted the picture, it had recently been the venue for the wedding of the Duke of York, the future George V. Its impressive facade, between St. James's Park and the area populated by gentlemen's clubs, is still a familiar sight for civil servants and tourists alike.

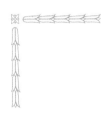

LONDON: ST. JAMES' PALACE.

PLATE 45

THE THAMES, CHARING CROSS

The Thames at Westminster was a much-painted view, unlike the scenes farther
down the river where ships unloaded the goods of the empire.

This view of the Houses of Parliament and Hungerford Bridge had already been made familiar by countless artists, particularly J. M. W. Turner, when Rose Barton made it the subject of one of her most colorful pictures. Turner's atmospheric style influenced the paintings of both James McNeill Whistler and his friend Claude Monet, who painted a spectacular series from the Savoy Hotel between 1899 and 1904. Rose Barton knew these painters and their work, and described wandering along Cheyne Walk, past the house where Turner had died on December 19, 1851.

Rose Barton's picture shows a peaceful and quiet Thames with two barges making their slow way downriver. In reality, it was an exceptionally busy river, particularly farther down, where the watermen could be found rowing workers from bank to bank and seamen to and from their ships. It was a hard life, with long hours and the constant danger of being run down by a passing steamer or capsized by a heavy barge. Surprisingly few watermen could swim, and many drowned. Young boys waded in the shallow water, picking up whatever they could find to take home or to sell for a few pennies.

The men worked as waterside laborers, loading and unloading heavy sacks of grain or bars of iron, crates of empty bottles and barrels of grease and fat; their wives worked as cleaners, or pulled the fur off rabbit skins. Even here, writers and painters like Whistler found a romantic ideal: "And when the evening mist clothes the riverside with poetry, as with a veil, and the poor buildings lose themselves in the dim sky, and the tall chimney become campanili, and the warehouses are palaces in the night, and the whole city hangs in the heavens, and fairyland is before us—then the wayfarer hastens home."

PLATE 46

TODDLERS

Benjamin Disraeli's *Sybil, or The Two Nations* was a subject of huge concern to many Victorian and Edwardian figures.

Where are the two little children going? What are they doing out at night? The two are moderately well-dressed, but photographs of the children in many of London's board schools show little girls in neat dresses with straw hats on their heads, even though they were from poor families.

Board schools had been set up following the Elementary Education Act of 1870, which provided education for the whole population. School boards were empowered to build and run schools where voluntary school places were lacking. In 1876, attendance was made compulsory and, in 1880, the school age was set from five to ten years old, though many schools had babies' classes for children of three years and up. The schools provided more than reading, writing, and arithmetic; they taught singing and practical lessons for girls in "housewifery"— managing a home, mending and "turning" garments to prolong their life, making their own metal and furniture polishes, and even making temporary blankets out of brown paper. Boys learned skills like woodworking.

Classes were crowded—about sixty children to one teacher—and some children were forced to bring their small brothers and sisters in with them. Some schools had underfed children, in others the children were too tired to learn, as they had been up at five in the morning to deliver milk, or had worked late in the evening selling papers. But the children were fed at school and taught the basics, giving the poorest the chance for a start in life.

PLATE 47

CROMWELL ROAD

Cromwell Road stretches west from the Victoria and Albert Museum to Earl's Court—a distance of about a mile.

Today Cromwell Road heaves with traffic and vibrates with noise while international hotels jostle for space with museums, but in 1850 the land on which it was built was still lush market gardens. Curiously, given that the road's name was chosen by Prince Albert—the husband of one of the most royal monarchs of them all, Queen Victoria—it celebrates the Puritan antimonarchist Oliver Cromwell who, as lord protector (a virtual dictator), lived in Hale House, where Cromwell Road now joins Queen's Gate.

The Natural History Museum, a symphony of Victorian variegated terra-cotta, spires, and towers, truly a "fitting storehouse for the wonders of creation," dominates the corner at Exhibition Road and can be seen on the right in this painting. Designed by Alfred Waterhouse, the spectacular building opened in 1881.

Inside today's museum, wonders really do abound. Dinosaurs roar realistically and an animatronic *Tyrannosaurus rex* uses its "senses" to spot prey—including unsuspecting humans. In the Earth Galleries, active volcano models erupt and earthquake machines shake. And in the newly developed Darwin Centre, Archie—a twenty-five-foot-long squid, captured alive off the Falklands but now dead—balefully looks out from a tank filled with formaldehyde. Other places of interest on Cromwell Road include the Victoria and Albert Museum and Baden Powell House—the Scout Association's international hostel and home to a museum celebrating Powell's life.

LONDON: THE VICTORIA AND ALBERT MUSEUM.

PLATE 48

ST. JAMES'S STREET: LEVEE DAY

Although Queen Victoria ended St. James's Palace's status as the monarch's official
residence in 1837, it remains a working palace to this day.

In Europe, a levee was a formal morning reception given by kings and other important members of the aristocracy. Louis XIV was awakened by his First Valet de Chambre at 8:30 a.m. and the levee or ceremonial rising began. First, doctors, family members, and current favorites were admitted to watch his majesty be washed, shaved, and combed; then, if it were a full levee day, he was dressed, and took a nourishing breakfast of broth before France's hundred or so most important officials were ushered in.

In Britain, the sovereign held afternoon levees at St. James's Palace. Far less elaborate than the old French ones, they were occasions for the sovereign to meet dignitaries. Only men were admitted and protocol was strict. Lord Nelson, after his resounding victory in the Battle of the Nile, was a hero throughout Europe, and when he returned to England was feted in the streets by the people. Despite this, because of his long-standing relationship with the married Emma Hamilton, he was shunned by George III at the royal levee of November 11, 1800. The first court appearance of the young Prince Albert, future husband of Queen Victoria, was at a levee day.

Although the custom of holding levees was discontinued at the start of World War II, St. James's Palace remains a working palace and the royal court is still formally based there. Although ambassadors are now received at Buckingham Palace, they are still accredited to the Court of St. James.

PLATE 49

SOUTH KENSINGTON STATION

First the underground steam railway, then the subway, took Londoners
below the streets in what was a quick but not necessarily comfortable journey.

Rose Barton's pictures tend to hark back to a more romantic capital than what was experienced by many Londoners, and this is her only picture of the underground railway that, by 1904, was so important to many of them. South Kensington Station was on the route of the Metropolitan District Railway, the world's first underground passenger railway, which began construction in 1860 and opened in 1863, carrying 40,000 passengers a day on trains that ran every ten minutes. By 1880, the expanded line carried 40 million passengers a year. The section from Paddington to South Kensington opened in 1868, with the District Line, soon followed by the Inner Circle, passing through the station. The original coaches were divided into first-, second-, and third-class compartments, the first class fitted with carpets, mirrors, and upholstered seats. Despite such comforts, the main problem of the underground steam railways was the supply of breathable air, though as Eric Banton wrote in *Living London* in 1901, "It is true that the sulphurous atmosphere is far from pleasant, but there is no reason to suppose that it is seriously injurious to health." Nonetheless, the lot of the engine drivers, the signalmen in their boxes at the end of the platforms, and the porters on duty was not a particularly happy or healthy one. One of the solutions was to bore "blow holes" as smoke vents to the roadways above, covering them with gratings, though this resulted in horses being startled when smoke and steam belched out from beneath them.

The underground railways, and the later, deeper subway lines, were essential to the growth of London. The lines passing through South Kensington were helped by the growing popularity of museums such as the Natural History Museum—which opened in 1881—and by exhibitions at the Victoria and Albert Museum. Earl's Court opened in 1887 with Buffalo Bill's Wild West Show and the District Line took full advantage, issuing combined rail and entry tickets.

PLATE 50

BROMPTON ROAD, LOOKING EAST

As fashionable now as it was in 1904, Brompton Road is now one of London's top "shop till you drop" destinations.

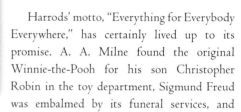

Brompton Road was once a tiny track that led to the hamlet of Brompton, known in the thirteenth century as Broom Farm. Now it is a wide, sweeping road that cuts through some of London's most exclusive and exorbitantly expensive real estate.

Harrods, its premier store, started life as a small grocery store owned by Charles Harrod in the village of Knightsbridge in 1849. Harrod soon expanded his stock to include medicines, perfumes, fruit, and stationery. By 1880, he was employing a hundred staff, and in 1889, Harrods became a public company. In 1927, the managing directors of Harrods and Oxford Street's Selfridges had a bet as to which store would make the most profit. Gordon Selfridge lost and presented Harrods with a large silver replica of its unique building.

Harrods' motto, "Everything for Everybody Everywhere," has certainly lived up to its promise. A. A. Milne found the original Winnie-the-Pooh for his son Christopher Robin in the toy department, Sigmund Freud was embalmed by its funeral services, and clients could even have their clocks wound at home by the store's specialty winding service.

Brompton Road used to have its own underground station, but it closed on July 29, 1934, because Knightsbridge Station, which had been rebuilt specifically to provide a direct link to Harrods, took the bulk of its business. The station was converted into the Royal Artillery's Anti-Aircraft Operations Room and used as such until 1955.

Now the station is ghostly—visits are not allowed on the grounds of safety and security. Several years ago, one curious individual attempted to gain entrance. His dead body was found at the bottom of a 110-foot-deep ventilation shaft. Apparently, he had fallen through from the roof above.

PLATE 51

CONSTITUTION HILL; THE BLUES

Constitution Hill is the processional road that runs from Buckingham Palace along the edge of Green Park
to Hyde Park corner, frequented by park keepers and perambulators in the summer,
and—as shown here—the Royal Horse Guards on wet, blustery days in the winter.

It was here, half a century before Rose Barton's painting, that prime minister Sir Robert Peel was fatally injured by a fall from his horse. Queen Victoria herself faced no less than three assassination attempts as she drove this way, alongside the wall of Buckingham Palace garden. Nobody has ever explained how the hill got its name, though there are suggestions that Charles II took his "constitutional" walks here.

The troop is from the Royal Horse Guards, one of the oldest regiments in the British Army, also known as the Blues because of the color of their uniforms. They were the creation of Charles II, their "Royal" epithet a reward for the part they played in protecting him during the dangerous years for the monarchy after its Restoration in 1660.

In 1892, the Blues had just returned from South Africa and the horrors of the Boer War. Rose Barton painted the troop riding through the drizzle, just past the Wellington Arch, at what was then its new position at the top of Constitution Hill. This was before the arch acquired the giant statue that dominates it today, *Peace Descending on the Quadriga of War*, which was placed there in 1912. The Blues must have passed the arch with pride: they covered themselves with glory under the Duke of Wellington at the Battle of Waterloo in 1815. They captured an eagle standard from one of Napoléon's regiments, and since then have worn a small eagle on their shoulders in recognition of that achievement.

PLATE 52

VILLIERS STREET, CHARING CROSS

Villiers Street is still a bustling thoroughfare: Samuel Johnson's words "I think the full tide of human existence is at Charing Cross" are as true today as they were when he wrote them.

Villiers Street is built on the estate of George Villiers, Duke of Buckingham (1592–1628), which was known as York House. Villiers, although a favorite of Charles I, incurred the wrath of Parliament for his inept handling of the war in France and for arranging Charles's marriage to a Catholic. Villiers was assassinated in 1628, but his dashing and courtly life was later immortalized as the romantic interest in Alexandre Dumas's famous book *The Three Musketeers.*

Villiers's estate was sold to property developers, and in 1674, Nicolas Barbon—the son of one of his old parliamentary enemies—razed the estate to the ground and created fashionable coffee houses and inns to cater to the burgeoning middle classes. In the 1860s, the west side of Villiers Street was demolished to make way for Charing Cross Station—a portal to far-flung and exotic places. It was from here that Phileas Fogg—hero of Jules Verne's *Around the World in 80 Days*—set out in 1872, ensconced in a first-class carriage, his incredulous manservant Passepartout by his side. Rudyard Kipling, fresh from India, resided at No. 43 from 1889 to 1891, and it was there that he wrote his most important work for adults, *The Light that Failed*—a tragic story of a man deserted by his love when he became blind.

LONDON: CHARING CROSS AND STRAND.

PLATE 53

FLEET STREET

Once the center of Britain's press, Fleet Street has returned to its origins—
that of an ordinary thoroughfare connecting the City to Westminster.

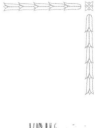

Fleet Street is named after the nearby underground river Fleet, which rises in the high ground of Hampstead and Kenwood and flows through the city to the Thames. Fleet Street's association with printing began around 1500, when the appropriately named Wynkyn de Worde moved there from William Caxton's old house in Westminster and printed a staggering (for the time) 800 books.

March 11, 1702, saw the printing of the first newspaper, the *Daily Courant*, to be followed by the *Morning Chronicle*. Such papers later reported luridly on one of Fleet Street's most famous characters—Sweeney Todd, the demon barber. Todd set up shop at No. 186 and dispatched over 150 customers. While they sat in his barber's chair, a trapdoor plunged these unfortunates to the

cellar below, where Todd slit their throats. Margery Lovett, a girlfriend of Todd's, had a pie shop nearby, which the lovers had discovered was linked to Todd's cellar by an ancient underground tunnel. In a perfect partnership, Todd's victims were transmuted into Lovett's freshly baked pies. Todd was hung on January 25, 1802; Lovett was found poisoned in her cell at Newgate Prison.

The journalists and printers of Fleet Street were hard drinkers—a fact reflected in the large number of pubs that, then as now, crowd the area. The Punch Tavern, originally the Crown and Sugarloaf, was once a glittering and magnificent gin palace—all mirrors, marble, and sparkle—built by the Baker brothers in 1893. The Old Bell, built in 1670, still serves the thirsty with ale, as does the gloomy Olde Cheshire Cheese, rebuilt after the Great Fire and frequented by individuals as diverse as Charles Dickens and Theodore Roosevelt.

Fleet Street dominated the newspaper business until Rupert Murdoch decamped to Wapping with the *Sun*, the *News of the World*, and the *Times*. Not one major press establishment remains today. Murdoch, to add insult to injury, conducted a memorial service for the old Fleet Street newspapers in St. Bride's in June 2005.

PLATE 54

THE LADY IN WAITING

Of all the children's illustrators, the most influential for untold generations was Kate Greenaway.

The little girl sitting on an uncomfortable chair, looking distinctly annoyed, could have been dressed in one of the Liberty of London's Kate Greenaway–inspired dresses that were proving so popular with the middle classes. Even the French adopted the style. Kate Greenaway's books and illustrations dominated Victorian and Edwardian nurseries, and her images of childhood—picking blackberries, blowing bubbles, or tossing balls in a never-ending pastoral delight, became the Victorian ideal of childhood.

The daughter of a master engraver and a skilled seamstress, Kate Greenaway studied at the Slade School of Art and began her career designing greeting cards and sketching for the *Illustrated London News*. Advances in printing brought mass production to book publishing in the 1860s; better and more education created a new audience, and Greenaway's first book, *Under the Window: Pictures and Rhymes for Children*, published in 1879, was an instant best seller. The engraver, Edmund Evans, spared no expense, using four-color blocks to produce the delicate watercolors. He printed an exceptionally large number, but the first edition of 20,000 sold out and he immediately had to produce a second printing of 70,000. In 1884, *The Language of Flowers* was published, with half of the first edition of 19,500 going to the United States. A whole industry was born around Kate Greenaway, and wallpaper, plates, scarves, and dolls soon appeared for a seemingly insatiable market.

Kate Greenaway's own childhood was a happy one. She later recalled, "Living in that childish wonder is a most beautiful feeling—I can so well remember it. There was always something more—behind and beyond everything— to me, the golden spectacles were very, very big."

PLATE 55

TOTTENHAM COURT ROAD

Tottenham Court Road's reputation as a street for furniture stores started in the nineteenth century.

Tottenham Court Road originally ran from Oxford Street to Tottenham Court, north of the Euston Road. It was known for the open-air market in nearby Whitecross Street, the stalls lit by oil lamps or candles stuck inside carved-out turnips, mainly selling food but also old shoes and new shirts, cutlery, and pans. The street's rural nature was still evident in 1840 when John Harris Heal took out the lease on land belonging to Capper's Farm for his new store, and had to provide for "the proper accommodation of 40 cows at least." The cowsheds burned down in 1877.

Heal & Son Ltd. became a household name in Britain when Ambrose Heal joined the firm in the late nineteenth century. His simple, beautiful, and functional arts and crafts furniture was instantly popular. "Everywhere it is pure simplicity and calmness," enthused the catalog from the 1900 Paris Exhibition, describing his award-winning designs. Even more important was its accessibility—here was superb furniture produced in quantity at reasonable prices, though the English reaction to his success was, typically, one of confusion. Furniture maker Gordon Russell later wrote, "By many craftsmen he was distrusted because he was in charge of an efficient business. By most businessmen he was regarded as a long-haired chap with odd notions."

Tottenham Court Road saw a second important arrival in 1841 when John Maple and a partner set up as wholesale and retail cloth dealers, cabinetmakers, and furnishing warehousemen. Soon they were able to offer "ten thousand Bedsteads in 600 styles for immediate delivery." Twelve years later, from a rebuilt store, Maples was supplying furniture to everyone from Queen Victoria to princes in India and the tsar in Russia. In 1905, Maples opened a branch in Paris and in the 1930s it claimed to be "the largest furniture establishment in the world."

Heal & Son, though no longer a family-owned store, continues to prosper today, but Maples has been replaced by a large electronics business.

PLATE 56

THREE LITTLE DUCKS

Nothing, it seems, could disturb the world of this small, self-confident child watching the ducks in a London park.

The young figure in Rose Barton's picture, in a pink coat and dress with a white bonnet and little boots, represented an idyll far removed from the reality of poor children, most of whom had to work from an early age. The poor wore well-darned, patched, and mismatched hand-me-downs; this little figure is carefully dressed, with layers hidden beneath the outer garments that could be astonishingly complicated. Around 1880, a child might be dressed in layers that included a vest; a knee-length calico chemise; wadded stays down the back with buttons around the waist for drawers, stocking suspenders, and a flannel petticoat; long stockings; and over all a white petticoat with a bodice.

Children's fashions were as important a part of life then as they are now, both for middle-class parents and for the retailers whose profits depended on the latest trends. Anything the royal family did was slavishly and instantly copied, so in came pleated skirts for boys in 1849 when a painting of the Prince of Wales in a Scottish kilt appeared, and "Scotch" suits were worn from 1850 to the 1870s. In turn, knickerbocker suits, an idea imported from the United States, gave way to sailor suits, selling by the thousands in the 1880s. Hats were de rigueur, for girls either a little bonnet or lavish flower- and ribbon-trimmed hats. Berets and tam-o'-shanters topped with a stylish pom-pom were also popular.

Kate Greenaway's effect on children's fashion was immediate. In her pictures, children are dressed in a style that was more Regency than Victorian: smock frocks for the boys and high-waisted pinafores, dresses, mobcaps, and straw bonnets for the girls. Liberty's of London used Greenaway's drawings as designs for the children's clothes it sold to well-to-do families.

PLATE 57

HAMMERSMITH 'BUS

Horses were vital in the explosive growth of public transportation in the nineteenth century, but in the early 1900s, motorized vehicles became more common, heralding the end of horse power.

On July 4, 1829, George Shillibeer, a coach builder and livery stable keeper in Bury Street, Bloomsbury, started the first regular bus service from Paddington via Regent's Park to Bank, a journey that took about an hour. The new form of transportation did not originate in England. Shillibeer had seen the omnibus in Paris, and his first vehicles were advertised as "a new carriage on the Parisian Mode." The name "omnibus" came from Nantes in France, where a Monsieur Omnes adopted the Latin pun on his own name for his horse-drawn company, calling it the Omnes omnibus ("All for everyone"). Shillibeer's bus carried around twenty passengers and was drawn by three horses. The idea caught on fast, and by the 1840s, they had completely replaced the old short stagecoach rides; the passengers hailed a bus from the roadside or banged on the roof to stop them. Horse-drawn buses were popular with those who could not afford a private carriage or an automobile.

Seats on both horse-drawn and motor buses remained significantly cheaper "on the top" until 1925, when the first covered-top bus appeared. And where else, as Gladstone famously remarked, could one see London and London life so well as from the top of a London bus. Shillibeer himself, in the face of intense competition, went bankrupt. Forced to adapt, he converted his omnibuses into "Shillibeer's Funeral Coaches" and went into the undertaking business.

By 1900, about 50,000 horses were pulling the different vehicles that took Londoners to work and play, producing approximately a thousand tons of manure a day, which was collected by dung carts and put on huge heaps before being sent to market gardens like those in the Lee Valley in Essex. The dirt was incredible, necessitating the "crossing sweepers," children and old men who earned tips sweeping a path in front of wealthy pedestrians. Horse-drawn buses were used by independent operators up to 1914.

PLATE 58

NELSON'S COLUMN, AND PORTICO OF ST. MARTIN'S-IN-THE-FIELDS

Nelson—hero of the Battle of Trafalgar—gazes down Whitehall from atop his 169-foot column in Trafalgar Square.

Nelson's Column, funded by public donations, was completed in 1842, and the twelve-foot statue was erected a year later. In Trafalgar Square—remodeled by architect John Nash in 1840—there could be no forgetting Britain's imperial grandeur. Each side of the pedestal supporting the column depicts one of Nelson's victories, four lions surround the memorial, and in 1900, three of the square's statues commemorated military commanders who extended Britain's imperial reach around the globe. (The fourth, visible in the painting, is of King George IV.)

Dissent plays an equally significant role in the story of Trafalgar Square. The square has hosted countless political meetings and rallies. Chartists demonstrated here in the 1840s, suffragettes in the 1900s, poll tax protestors in the 1990s.

The present church of St. Martin-in-the-Fields (the modern spelling) is the third, the first being a small chapel built by the monks of Westminster Abbey who came to work here in their convent garden in the Middle Ages. The one we see today, and that Rose Barton knew, was designed by James Gibbs and completed in 1726. St. Martin-in-the-Fields has had its fair share of associations with the famous: Charles II was christened here in 1630; burials include the Elizabethan miniature painter Nicholas Hilliard, Nell Gwynne in 1687, highwayman Jack Sheppard, and cabinetmaker Thomas Chippendale. "The Fields" refers to the countryside that surrounded the first medieval church on the site, used by the monks of Westminster.

PLATE 59

BELL INN, HOLBORN

The Old Bell Inn was another of those corners of lost medieval London that Rose Barton wanted to preserve for posterity.

Here it is, a ramshackle place with a black cat, long past its days of glory. In fact, the Old Bell at 123 Holborn, together with its extraordinary galleries around the courtyard, had disappeared entirely by 1900. It had been pulled down, ready for the enormous upheaval of redevelopment that was already taking shape in the area as Rose Barton's book of pictures was published; changes included a new streetcar interchange at Holborn Kingsway.

A century before, Holborn was packed with inns and pubs that also acted as transportation interchanges on the way into London. Stagecoaches from all over the Midlands and the south and west of England would arrive at the Bell and other inns along Holborn at set times each day. Regular travelers often rented rooms here before going on into London the next morning. Archbishop Robert Leighton, saintly and reluctantly taking up the position of one of Charles II's new bishops in Scotland, who always said that it was his ambition to die in an inn, had his wish granted when he died at the Bell in 1684. Earlier that same century, Shakespearian actors would have performed to audiences thronging the balconies, just as they did at the George Inn in Southwark, one of the only balconied inns in London to survive Rose Barton's generation.

By 1904, travelers from Leighton's home in Sussex would have taken an hour or so to travel, via the green and brass liveried trains of the South Eastern & Chatham Railway, into Charing Cross. They would then have crossed the city in one of the 2,500 horse-drawn buses that filled the streets of London.

PLATE 60

ST. MARTIN'S-IN-THE-FIELDS

St. Martin-in-the-Fields is home to the London Brass Rubbing Centre and hosted the first
radio broadcast of a church service under the charismatic Dick Sheppard in 1924.

The first mention of St. Martin's-in-the-Fields dates to 1222: a tiny chapel surrounded by fields and used by the monks of Westminster. Henry II built a new church on the site and extended the parish boundaries to prevent plague victims from being carried through his palace. Plague was rife in fifteenth- and sixteenth-century England—an epidemic killed about 20,000 people in 1499–1500—and Catherine of Aragon, Henry VIII's first wife, announced that although she was no prophet, she feared greatly for his life.

The church is now a landmark. Rebuilt between 1722 and 1726, it is a supreme example of the architecture of James Gibb and has been much copied across the United States. It is also famous worldwide for its humanitarian and practical brand of Christianity. Dick Sheppard, vicar from 1914 to 1927, saw St. Martin's as "the church of the ever open door" and gave shelter to homeless soldiers returning from France in World War I. St. Martin's continues to dedicate itself to helping the homeless, the lost, and the hungry of London, whatever their creed or nationality, and was instrumental in founding the charitable organizations Shelter and the Big Issue.

Known for its regular program of concerts, many by candlelight, the church also has a crypt with a brass rubbing center and an on-site café.

Plate 61

WATERLOO BRIDGE

The bustle, noise, and smog-reflecting light of the river Thames was one of the most characteristic sights of London in the early part of the twentieth century.

Rose Barton's painting of the river, from the Victoria Embankment below Waterloo Bridge, was executed just a few years before one of the most famous series of London paintings ever made. From 1899 to 1904, the great French impressionist Claude Monet painted nearly a hundred scenes from the fifth-floor balcony of his room at the Savoy Hotel, only yards from this spot. "Without the fog," he said, "London would not be a beautiful city." The same sense of fog and smoke is captured here, with the same distant view of Big Ben upstream.

The hundreds of steps down to the river, from one side of London to the other, which had once provided access to thousands of small boats along the river, were less used in Rose Barton's day. But the tugs, ferries, and barges dashed backward and forward as energetically as ever, although the big ships came no farther upstream than Tower Bridge and the docks.

Waterloo Bridge itself was finished in 1817, two years after the famous battle for which it was named. It required constant repairs, and by the time Rose Barton painted it, there were discussions about pulling it down and replacing it. This was eventually done during World War II, but not before three Hollywood films had been made, all called *Waterloo Bridge* and all set just a few years after this scene was painted.

MAPS OF LONDON

In 1902, George Philip and Son published *Philips' Handy-Volume Atlas of London*. This consisted of fifty-five sectional maps in color on a scale of three inches to the mile, and twelve special maps and plans, such as a plan of Westminster Abbey. It also included a directory of public buildings, as well as information about railways, tramways, and steamboats. We have reproduced eight of these maps—plate numbers 15, 16, 17, 22, 23, 24, 29, and 30—which cover central London (see the index map below) and all of the locations of Rose Barton's paintings.

Captions and notes for the map section can be found on page 174.

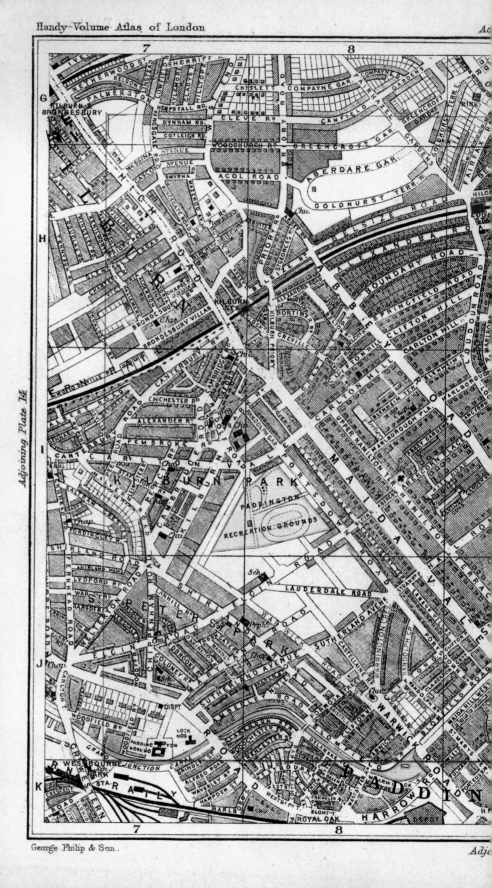

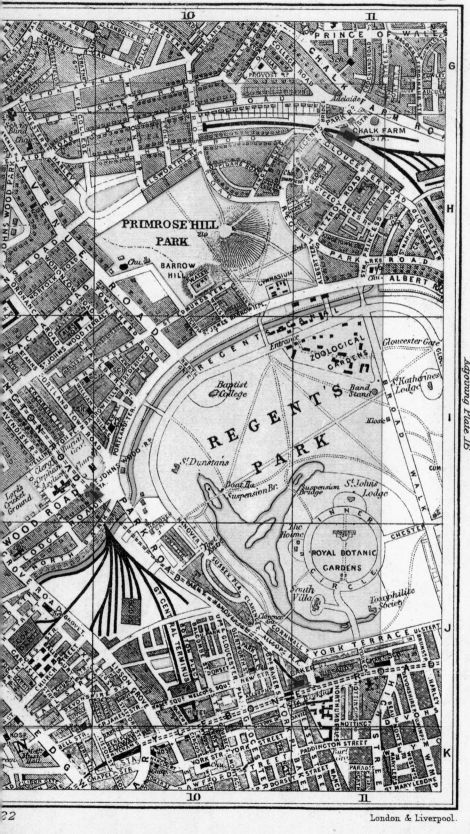

Plate 15

Plan of the
ZOOLOGICAL GARDENS.

London & Liverpool.

Adjoining Plate 15

Plate 16

London & Liverpool.

Plate 17

London & Liverpool.

Adjoining Plate 21

GREAT WESTERN RAILWAY
Ticket for a Bicycle, Perambulator, or Chair
Mail Cart with Passenger at Owner's Risk.
PADDINGTON (1 B.) TO
any G.W. Station not exceeding 75 miles
CARRIAGE PAID 1/6
This Ticket must given up on arrival
See other side

146

LONDON : KENSINGTON PALACE. DUTCH GARDENS.

George Philip & Son.

152

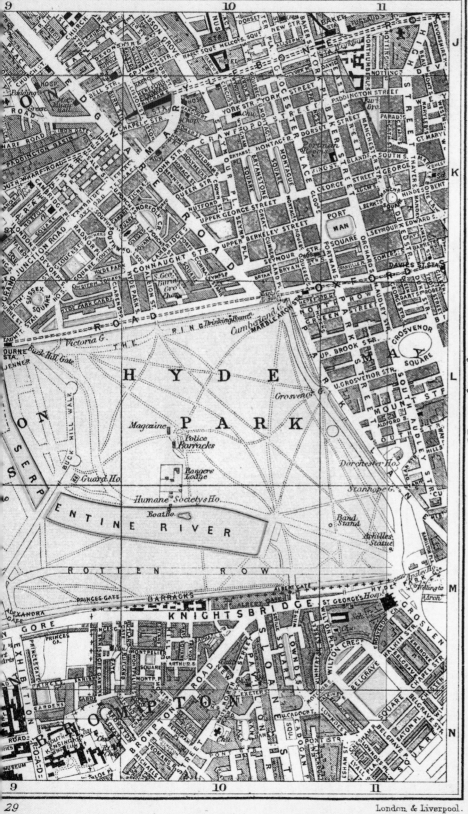

LONDON: MARBLE ARCH.

LONDON THE ALBERT MEMORIAL.

LONDON: THE BRITISH MUSEUM.

D. 4249 LONDON: LAW COURTS.

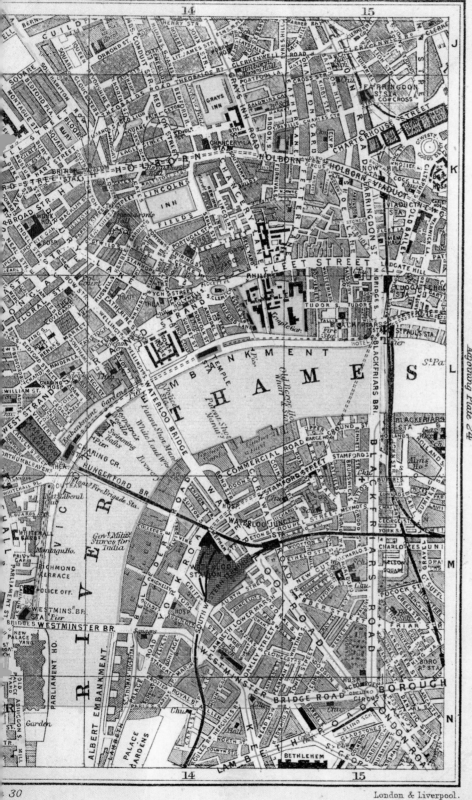

Plate 23

THAMES

RIVER

C. 34807. LONDON: WESTMINSTER ABBEY.

C. 43373. LONDON. WESTMINSTER BRIDGE & ST. THOMAS' HOSPITAL.

C. 40518. LONDON. ST PAULS CATHEDRAL.

C. 36749. LONDON BRIDGE.

Adjoining Plate 23

George Philip & Son.

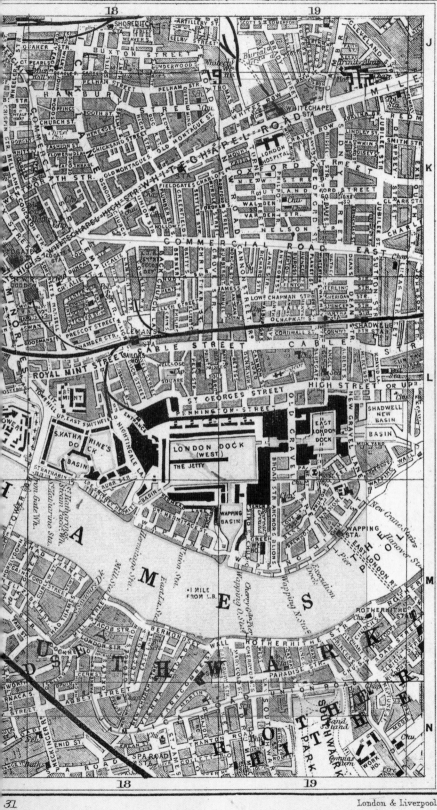

Plate 24

Adjoining Plate 25

London & Liverpool.

LONDON. THE TOWER—WHITE TOWER

George Philip & Son.

Plate 22

Plate 29

Adjoining Plate 30

London & Liverpool.

LONDON: WESTMINSTER CATHEDRAL.

LONDON: THE TATE GALLERY.

Adjoining Plate 29

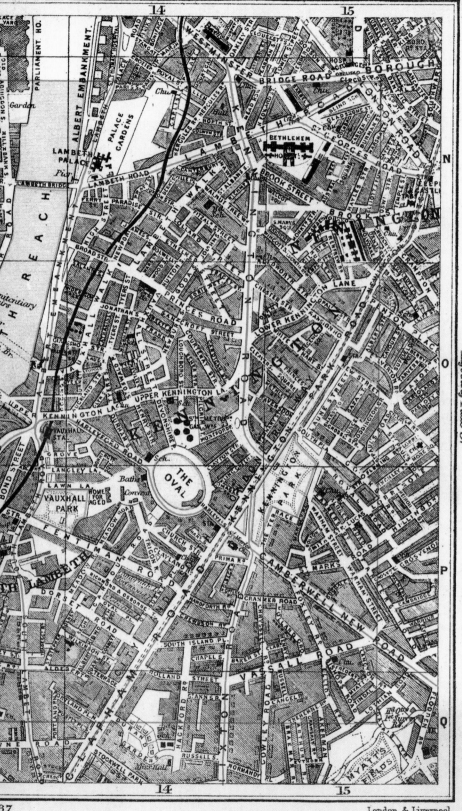

Adjoining Plate 31

11218. LONDON, LAMBETH PALACE.

About the Original Book

By 1905, when *Familiar London* was published, A&C Black had issued thirty books in the 20 Shilling Series of color plate books. Most depicted and described foreign countries, unfamiliar and exotic places to the reader of the early 1900s: Burma, India, Kashmir, Egypt, Japan, and Morocco; or cities such as Florence, Naples, and Rome. A selection of the books were by the founding artist of the series, Mortimer Menpes: *War Impressions, World Pictures, World's Children.* A few described places in Britain: *Bonnie Scotland, Beautiful Wales, The Channel Islands.* Still others depicted the works of well-known watercolorists, including Helen Allingham, Kate Greenaway, and George Cruikshank.

The series itself had already proven a success and went some way to restoring the fortunes of the publisher, which had fallen on hard times during the late nineteenth century. With between sixty and ninety illustrations produced by a three-color (sometimes four-color) mechanical process and a boldly decorated cover, they filled a gap in the market even at the high price of £1 per copy. Most had an initial print run of 3,000 copies, and many were frequently reprinted.

No records remain to tell us why, in late 1903, A&C Black decided to add four books on London to the series. A letter of October 1903 offered the Irish-born, London-based artist Rose Barton £200 for the right to reproduce seventy-five illustrations (she seems to have produced only sixty-one, though there is no indication of whether she was paid less in consequence) and £50 for 50,000–60,000 words of text, not necessarily to be written by her. The publisher's publication book, however, quotes a total figure of £300 paid.

The text, which Rose decided to write herself, gave some problems. "Dear Madam," Adam Black wrote in April 1904, "We think the MS is improved & trust the rest will be kept up to the same level. We would suggest that when complete it be put in the hands of an expert reviser." The published text runs to just under 40,000 words, well below the requested total. Possibly the reviser cut it heavily.

The title was also in dispute: "Do you not think we might yet hit upon a more flowing title? How would 'Aspects of London' do? What is wanted is a title of the same style as 'Happy England' & 'Bonnie Scotland' . . . What about 'Vistas of London'?"

The book was finally published in November 1904 with the title *Familiar London* in an edition of 3,000 copies plus a large paper limited edition of 300 copies signed by Rose Barton. The cover design was by A. A. Turbayne, whose work is featured in most of the series; his trademark scarab can be seen at the lower left on the front cover.

Both paintings and words were well received by contemporary critics, the words "providing a valuable insight into the life of a painter working in London and her favourite haunts," whereas the paintings were said to show a "true appreciation of the varied and beautiful colours of the metropolis."

A New World of Color Printing

The late Victorians and Edwardians loved color, and great strides in printing and ink technology allowed them to have it, breaking free of the limitations of the monotone pages of their parents' generation with their woodcuts and steel engravings. Many of these developments came from Germany where, by the turn of the nineteenth century, there was a lucrative industry in color postcards, greeting cards, and books containing dozens of color illustrations.

The challenge and promise of color were quickly taken up in Britain, where presses—especially in London and Edinburgh—started to use the latest technology to print color plates for a range of reference books.

Until the early 1890s, anyone wanting to print a color image had to design the images in such a way that the different colors, each printed from its own plate, could easily be separated from each other. Many ways were developed to create subtlety in the

The preface to the 1904 ninth edition of *Alpine Flora* (left), written by L. Schröter and Professor Doctor C. Schröter, boasts that "special attention has once more been given to the execution of the illustrations, which are much improved."

use of color, including engraving fine detail into each color plate, using separate plates for different tones of the same color, and finishing each plate by hand after it had been printed. Even so, most color printing in 1900 was fairly crude, and it is clear—especially under the magnifying glass—that the drive for realistic color still had some way to go.

The photograph of Hackfell Glen in Yorkshire (far left) was produced in 1909 in two printings by a process that was known as "rainbow" printing.

An Appetising Lunch (above), an image created by John Swain and Son, from the *Penrose Pictorial Annual* of 1906–7. The still life (right) is from the same source. The Hentschel advertisement (far right) was printed in the 1904–5 *Penrose Pictorial Annual*.

The chromographoscope, invented by Louis Ducos du Hauron in 1874, was a dual-purpose machine. It could be used as a camera or as an additive viewer.

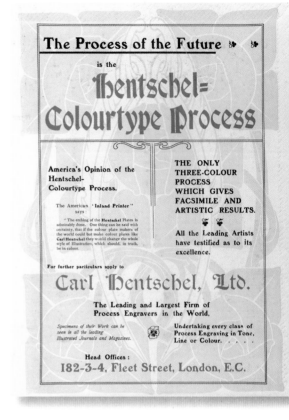

The Process of the Future is the **Hentschel Colourtype Process**

America's Opinion of the Hentschel Colourtype Process.

The American "Inland Printer" says:

"The etching of the **Hentschel** Plates is admirably done. One thing can be said with certainty, that if the colour plate makers of the world could but make colour plates like **Carl Hentschel** they would change the whole style of Illustration, which should, in truth, be in colour."

THE ONLY THREE-COLOUR PROCESS WHICH GIVES FACSIMILE AND ARTISTIC RESULTS.

All the Leading Artists have testified as to its excellence.

For further particulars apply to

Carl Hentschel, Ltd.

The Leading and Largest Firm of Process Engravers in the World,

Specimens of their Work can be seen in all the leading Illustrated Journals and Magazines.

Undertaking every class of Process Engraving in Tone, Line or Colour. . . . .

Head Offices: **182-3-4, Fleet Street, London, E.C.**

The best color printing in 1900, however, was stunning. In the period between 1900 and 1914, before war dried up ink and machinery supplies from Germany to the rest of the world, printing in color reached a peak that was not to be reached again until the 1960s.

How was this quality achieved? It is important to remember that outdoor color photography as we know it, using color film to photograph places and people, was not invented until the 1930s. However, from about 1890 onward, several processes for making color photographs of inanimate objects in a studio setting were well advanced, and Edwardian photographers were amazingly inventive.

One of the greatest pioneers was a German emigrant, Carl Hentschel, who in the 1890s patented the Hentschel Colourtype Process and set up his company on London's Fleet Street. Hentschel developed a massive camera that used three color filters—red, green, and blue—to capture simultaneous images of any original flat color image. At the same time, developments such as the halftone screen, which allowed color gradation to be printed as an almost-imperceptible pattern of different-sized dots onto paper, were enabling photographed images to be transferred to paper, both in black and white and in the new three-color process.

It was now possible to photograph flat objects like paintings—or small groups of objects in a studio setting—in color. And it was possible to use those images, separated into their three component process colors, to print color images. It was impossible, however, to make color photographs of the wide outside world, of cities, mountains, and crowds of people. Yet once they had a taste of color postcards and color pictures in books, those who could afford to buy such relatively expensive luxuries wanted as much color as they could get.

The images in this book demonstrate the many ways in which Edwardian inventors, photographers, and publishers strove to give their customers what they so craved—the real world on the printed page in full color.

The Hentschel Three-Color Process

In 1868, when he was four years old, Carl Hentschel moved to London from the Russian-Polish city of Lodz with his family. Like his father, he became an engraver, and by 1900 was an important figure in color printing and in London's social life. As well as being an active advocate of his innovative printing process, he was a founding member of several clubs, including the Playgoer's Club and, as a great friend of Jerome K. Jerome, was the model for Harris in Jerome's *Three Men in a Boat.*

Carl Hentschel (top left) and the original three men in a boat (below)—Carl Hentschel, George Wingrave, and Jerome K. Jerome. The portrait of a lady (below left) was reproduced using the three-color process, and appeared in *Colour Printing and Colour Printers* by R. Burch, published in 1910. The photograph of the house (below) is an example of three-color halftone reproduction, and appeared in the same book.

Although not the inventor of the three-color halftone process—it had been developed by Frenchmen Louis du Hauron and Charles Cros and American Frederick Ives in the 1870s—Hentschel's company led the way in using the method on a commercial scale.

The process is well described in Burch's 1906 book *Colour Printing and Colour Printers*: "Once the principle is accepted that any combination of colours can be resolved into its primary elements, it remains only for the photographer to obtain three negatives which automatically dissect the original, making three distinct photographic records of the reds, yellows and blues which enter into the composition. The result is obtained by the use of transparent screens of coloured pigment or liquid, 'light filters' as they are technically termed, placed in front of the lens. These filters admit any two of the primary colours and absorb the other one. Three separate screens are employed, each with the lines ruled at a different angle, and when the negative records of the colour analysis are obtained, the three photographs are converted into printing surfaces."

Among Hentschel's growing list of customers was Adam Black, the original "A" of A&C Black, who early on recognized the Colourtype process as the one that would give his publishing company a head start in the production of color books. In its time, it must have seemed magical that color plates could be produced to such a high standard and—at only four hours from photograph to finished printing plate—so quickly.

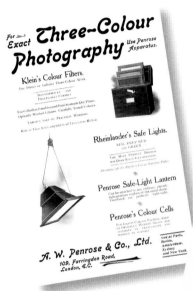

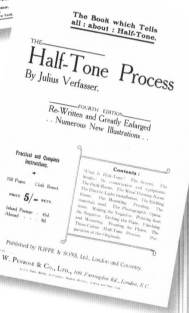

The *Penrose Pictorial Annuals* had an extensive section of advertisements at the end of each issue. The advertisement for three-color photography equipment comes from the 1906–7 edition, and the one for the halftone process book is from 1907–8. The painting by J. C. Hook (right), entitled *The Stream*, was reproduced in Burch's *Colour Printing and Colour Printers* in 1910 as an example of the new screenless three-color process.

DISTRICT MESSENGERS RESERVING PLACES AT THE THEATRE

RED, WHITE & BLUE

By 1904, Raphael Tuck had more than 10,000 different postcard designs and had launched its Oilette brand, based on original and often very beautiful paintings. There would eventually be more than 3,000 different sets of Tuck Oilette postcards. Tuck's range included many postcards taken from illustrations in the A&C Black books, and A&C Black itself published a similar quantity of postcards under its own name.

COLOR POSTCARDS

The first decade of the twentieth century was the high tide of the postcard craze, which used the new technologies of color printing and the halfpenny postcard postage rate to fill Edwardian living rooms with pictures from all over the world. In 1899, the British Post Office gave in to popular pressure to allow postcards to have more than just the address written on the back, which allowed publishers to use all of the picture side to display their design.

Postcard publishers rapidly increased production to fill the demand for postcards, these cards being the one

product line that constantly pushed color printing to the limits of what was achievable. Many color postcards, even of out-of-the-way British scenes, were printed in Germany, or by British companies with German origins. None was more inventive, productive, and formative than the London-based company of Raphael Tuck and Sons. Raphael Tuch (his original name) moved to London with his wife and eleven children from Breslau in Prussia in 1865. He opened a small shop in Whitechapel, moving in 1870 to City Road, where he and his sons Adolph, Herman, and Gustave helped develop a range of photographs and Victorian scraps, much of it imported from Germany. In 1871 came the first Christmas card, and in 1876

WESTMINSTER. HOUSES OF PARLIAMENT.

The Raphael Tuck colophon (center) for the Artistic Series of postcards. The postcard (left) was mailed in London on June 7, 1905, by a mother to her son at school in Filey, Yorkshire.

the colored oleograph. The breakthrough year for the postcard was 1894, when Tuck produced a card with a vignette of Snowdon in North Wales.

In the first decades of the postcard's life, there were three ways of producing a color image. You either started with a real black-and-white photograph and added subtle layers of color to indicate water or a sunset, used traditional color engravers to create separated color designs from scratch, or used the new three-color process to photograph painted originals. It was this third option that allowed companies like Raphael Tuck and Sons to expand so rapidly, and they were quick to commission a number of excellent artists to create series of paintings specifically for reproduction as postcards.

PHOTOCHROMES

Of all the methods for colorizing photographic images before outdoor color photography, the photochrome process was probably the most successful. The brilliantly colored prints displayed at the 1889 Paris Exposition by the Swiss company Orell Füssli and Co. won a gold medal, and their realism thrilled those who saw them. Only three companies—Füssli's own Photoglob in Switzerland, Photochrome in Britain, and the Detroit Printing Company in the United States—were ever licensed to use the "secret" technique, which by 1910 had resulted in more than 13,000 color images of every corner of Europe and the landmarks of North America, India, and North Africa.

Each photochrome required intensive labor, an artistic eye, and, ideally, an accurate record of what colors were actually present in the scene portrayed. A film negative was used as the basis for creating a series of lithographic plates—flat pieces of stone quarried in

Piccadilly Circus in the West End of London (below) is shown as a relatively sedate and formal place in this photochrome image. It contrasts with the crowded bustle of the East End's Petticoat Lane (far right) on a Sunday morning.

Bavaria and coated with asphaltum, one stone for each color. The negative had to be retouched by hand for each color, sometimes with fourteen different colors being used, then the stone exposed to sunlight for several hours before it was developed with turpentine. Each stone was hand-finished with the additional development of chosen areas and fine pumice powder before being etched in acid to reveal the image ready for printing. Special semitransparent inks were then used to transfer the image from the stones onto smooth paper, and finally each printed image was varnished to bring out its depth and richness.

The British Photochrom Company, with offices in London and Tunbridge Wells, published around 150 photochrome images of London, available to the public as prints for framing and as postcards. These and more than 5,000 other photochromes can be seen online at http://www.ushistoricalarchive. com/photochroms/index.html.

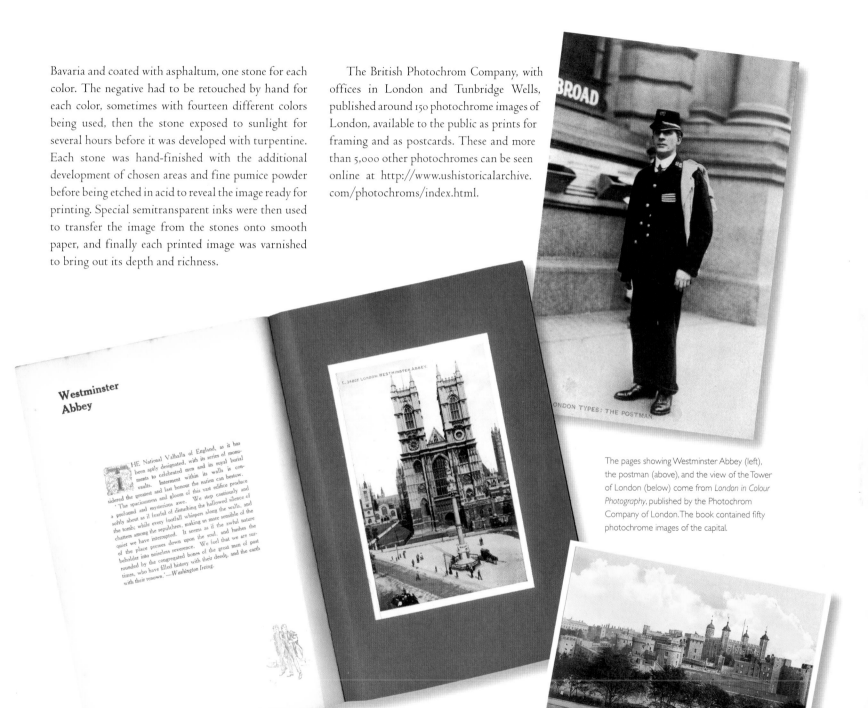

The pages showing Westminster Abbey (left), the postman (above), and the view of the Tower of London (below) come from *London in Colour Photography*, published by the Photochrom Company of London. The book contained fifty photochrome images of the capital.

When they launched the 20 Shilling Series of colored books in 1903, A&C Black knew full well that, in order to sell books at such a high price, the look of the book from the outside was just as important as the innovative color used on the inside.

American-born Albert Angus Turbayne moved to London in the early 1890s and established a close association with the pioneering bindery at the Carlton Studio. By 1903, his William Morris–inspired designs were considered to be the pinnacle of the bookbinder's art. His forte was the combination of exuberant blocking, often in three or four colors, and beautifully executed lettering, but one of the bindery's greatest skills was in creating designs that exactly matched the subject of the book. Albert Turbayne always did extensive research into his subject, consulting libraries and illustrated books to find precisely the right elements with which to illustrate each of the Black books.

The design details of the present series of *Memories of Times Past* books pay homage to the skills of the Turbayne Bindery. The designs in the side panels of the cover are derived from the original covers of the Black books, and the decorative elements within the book echo these designs, thus maintaining the theme and feel that Turbayne strove to achieve.

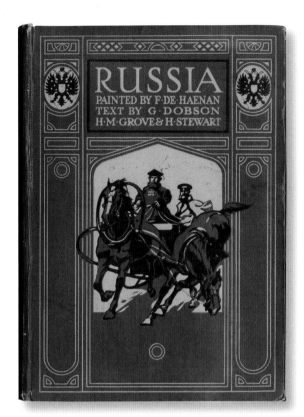

SOURCES, NOTES, AND CAPTIONS

The images used to complement the Rose Barton paintings come from a wide variety of sources, including books, postcards, museums, and libraries. They include photochromes, ephemera, advertisements, and maps of the period. The numbers refer to the plate numbers.

1 Prince Edward drilling his brother and sister (right) was painted by John Williamson and reproduced in *The Children's Book of London* in 1903. Their majesties' grandchildren entering Marlborough House (top left) is from *Living London*, Volume I, edited by George Sims in 1902. Whitehall (below left), with the trees in the grounds of Montague House visible on the right, was painted by Herbert Marshall and published in *The Scenery of London* in 1905.

2 The image of Westminster (top right) is from a painting by M. or W. Johnson, reproduced as a Tuck's Oilette postcard. A 1904 sovereign (left) sits over an image of Edward VII's coronation.

3 The splendor of the meeting of the Coaching Club at Hyde Park on the Wednesday after Derby day, to go to Hurlingham or Ranelagh, is captured in this painting reproduced in *London's Social Calendar*—a brochure produced by the Savoy Hotel and distributed to its patrons *c.* 1910. The photograph (top right) appeared in *401 Views of London*, published by W. H. Smith around 1912.

4 The two drawings of Rotten Row (top left and right) by Hugh Thomson are from *Highways and Byways in London*, published by Macmillan in 1902. The map showing Rotten Row is from the 1902 *Bacon's Up-to-Date Pocket Atlas and Guide to London*. A morning in Rotten Row (below right) is a photochrome from *London in Colour Photography*, published by the London Photochrom Company in about 1902.

5 E. W. Haslehust's painting of St. Paul's and Ludgate Hill (bottom right) was reproduced in *Beautiful London*, with text by Walter Jerrold. The photochrome (left) of the same view featured in *London in Colour Photography*. The photograph (top right) showing the railway viaduct very clearly is from *401 Views of London*.

6 The painting of Buckingham Palace gardens is by Mima Nixon, from *London* by A. R. Hope Moncrieff, published by A&C Black in 1916 (it was originally printed in the 1916 A&C Black title *Royal Palaces and Gardens*). The advertisement for umbrellas is from the 1904 Christmas edition of *Our Darlings*. The photochrome of Buckingham Palace is from *London in Colour Photography*.

7 *View Across the River from Hungerford Bridge* is a painting (center) by Yoshio Markino from *The Colour of London*, published by Chatto and Windus in 1914. The sketch (right) by Frants Henningsen was published in the 1904–5 edition of the *Penrose Pictorial Annual*. The viewpoint of the photograph (bottom left) is looking east from Hungerford Bridge. *Can You Keep a Secret?* is the title of the drawing (center), published in *Our Darlings* in 1906.

8 The image of the cabmen enjoying their lunch (center) in a cabman's shelter is from *Living London*, Volume 2, edited by George Sims in 1903. The images of cabs (below right) show a hansom (top) and a four-wheeler (below). John Williamson painted the cabman and his horse (below left). A cabman's wooden green shelter is visible behind the cab.

9 A Harrods van of 1904 (below right) sits over a textile sample from Liberty. A lady shopping in Knightsbridge (center) would have been familiar with the costume skirt of the period (below left).

10 The *Penrose Pictorial Annual* of 1909–10 featured an article by Chas E. Dawson entitled "Line Drawings for Newspaper Advertisements: The Selfridge Cartoons." The advertisement for the opening of Selfridges (left), drawn by Garth Jones, was included in this article and was one of a series that were printed on a full page "in the leading daily journals of London for a week." The two images (center) are of Oxford Street—the drawing is by L. G. Hornby, published by A&C Black in 1912 in *London, A Sketch Book*.

11 *The Playground of the Poor* is the title of the painting (bottom) by John Williamson from *The Children's Book of London* by G. E. Mitton, published by A&C Black in 1903. *Feeding the Pigeons* (top right) was published in the *Penrose Pictorial Annual* for 1904–5. *Feeding Pigeons in Hyde Park* (top left) is an illustration from *Living London*, Volume 2. The painting of the pigeon (below left) is from *The British Bird Book*, edited by F. B. Kirkman, published by T&E Jack in 1911.

12 The painting by Kate Greenaway (right) is entitled *Two Girls in a Garden*, and was reproduced in *Kate Greenaway* by Spielmann and Layard, published by A&C Black in 1905. The illustration of the daffodil is by Mabel E. Step from *Wayside and Woodland Blossoms*, published by Warne in 1906. The illustration from *Alice in Wonderland* (top left) is by Sir John Tenniel.

13 *A Conference* is the title of the painting (below left) reproduced in the *Penrose Pictorial Annual* of 1915. The Tucks postcard (top left) shows Piccadilly club land in London. Volume 1 of *Living London* included the image of an arrival at the Carlton Club (top right). The photograph (below) shows the complicated acrobatics involved in photographing at the Wallace Collection (which was apparently only allowed on Monday mornings). The photograph is from the *Penrose Pictorial Annual* of 1908–9.

14 Sailing yachts in Kensington Gardens (top right) and early morning swimmers in Hyde Park (center) both come from Volume 1 of *Living London*. The Serpentine boat house (top left) is from *401 Views of London*.

15 The main image of Hyde Park corner is a photochrome. Quadriga at Hyde Park corner (top) is from *401 Views of London*, as is the view (below) of Hyde Park corner from the park.

16 The panorama of Hyde Park corner (below) dates from 1909. The painting of Hyde Park corner (left) by Herbert Marshall is from *The Scenery of London*, published by A&C Black in 1905. The advertisement (right) for raincoats was produced by Frank Bentall of Kingston-on-Thames.

17 *Morning Parade by Rotten Row* is the title of the painting (below) by Yoshio Markino, published in *The Colour of London* by Chatto and Windus in 1914. Ladies walking in Hyde Park near Park Lane (center) comes from Volume 1 of *Living London*. The azalea (top) is from Thompson's *Gardener's Assistant*, Volume 2, published by the Gresham Publishing Company in 1900.

18 E. W. Haslehust painted the Lancaster Gate fountain in Kensington Gardens (below left), and the photochrome (top) shows the Round Pond in Kensington Gardens from *London in Colour Photography*. Peter Pan's statue in Kensington Gardens (far right) sits above the map featured on the endpapers of *J. M. Barrie's Peter Pan in Kensington Gardens*, retold by May Byron with pictures by Arthur Rackham, published by Hodder & Stoughton in 1920.

19 The Dog's Cemetery in Hyde Park (top right) as depicted in *Living London*, Volume 1. *Companions* is the title of the image (left) of the woman and her dog, reproduced in the *Penrose Pictorial Annual* of 1908–9. *Chatterbox*, an annual children's illustrated collection of stories, information, poetry, and activities, printed the dog and doll image, entitled *Treasure Trove*, in its 1906 edition. The *Penrose Pictorial Annual* of 1902 printed the doggy picture frame (center), entitled *All Sorts and Conditions*.

20 *A Gala Evening at Covent Garden Opera House* (below) was published in *London's Social Calendar*—a brochure produced by the Savoy Hotel for its patrons. The image of H.R.H. King Edward VII and Queen Alexandra was included in a coronation souvenir booklet produced with the compliments of R.W. Righton, Wholesale Retail and General Draper, Evesham, in 1902. The picture of Princess Louise, Duchess of Fife, is from the same source.

21 The daisy (top left) by Mabel E. Step is from *Wayside and Woodland Blossoms*, published in 1909 by Frederick Warne. *The Investiture of the Prince of Wales at Carnarvon Castle* (below left) is an image from a Kinemacolor film as printed in the *Penrose Pictorial Annual* of 1911–12. Prince Edward of York (right) and his family is from the coronation souvenir booklet, details of which are under plate 20, above.

22 "Gladstone Looking Very Severe" (top) in a photo from *Hutchinson's Story of the British Nation*, published by Hutchinson & Co. "Gladstone Introducing the Home Rule Bill on 13 February 1893" (center) is from the same source. *Speshul!* is the title of the drawing (below right) from *Highways and Byways in London*, published by Macmillan in 1902.

23 The original Royal Exchange (top left) in Cornhill, London, is from *London* by Walter Besant, published by Chatto and Windus in 1892. Two postcard views of the Royal Exchange (below)—the image on the left is a photochrome as published in *London in Colour Photography*.

24 Smithfield Market (top left), from *Ryman's Handy Handbook of London* published by G. Falkner & Sons. Of the two similar views of Cloth Fair, the image on the left is from *London* by A. R. Hope Moncrieff, published by A&C Black in 1916. The drawing (right) is from *Highways and Byways in London*, published by Macmillan in 1902.

25 The single rose (right) is a painting entitled *Gathering*, created by the Carlton Studio and published in the *Penrose Pictorial Annual* of 1912–13. Yoshio Markino painted *The Flower Sellers in Piccadilly Circus* (left). The wonderful flower seller (center) is a photochrome as published in *London in Colour Photography*.

26 The thatched cottage (right) was painted by Philip Norman in 1895 and published in *London Vanished and Vanishing* by A&C Black in 1905. It illustrates another loss of rurality in London: this cottage was situated behind number 12 St. Marys Terrace, Paddington Green, and was demolished in 1897. The photograph (top) shows modern-day Glebe Place in Chelsea.

27 *Whistler's Nocturne Blue and Silver—Chelsea 1871* (top), and *Chelsea* (below), as painted by Herbert Marshall in *The Scenery of London*.

28 A lamp cleaner (top left) and a lamp-repair shop (below) belonging to the South Metropolitan Gas Company, as featured in Volume 3 of *Living London*. Yoshio Markino's evocative painting of Chelsea Embankment in the rain (center) matches the mood of *The Derelict*, painted by Harry W. Whanslaw in 1906, showing the same distinctive lamps, and produced as a two-color print in the *Penrose Pictorial Annual* of 1907–8.

29 The photograph of the statue of Thomas Carlyle in Chelsea (center) is from *401 Views of London*, and the portrait of Carlyle (right) is by James Whistler. The drawing of Carlyle's home at 24 Cheyne Row is from *Ryman's Handy Handbook of London*, published by G. Falkner & Sons.

30 A selection of garden instuments to catch insects (left) and an old map of the Chelsea Physic Garden (center). Chelsea Physic Garden as it is today (right).

31 The map (below) is from *Bacon's Up-to-Date Pocket Atlas and Guide to London*, dated 1902. The colorful cyclist (left) is from the cover of a bicycle catalog by John Swain and Sons, as reproduced in the *Penrose Pictorial Annual* of 1906–7. Herbert Marshall painted Battersea Reach (center) from opposite Turner's house at 119 Cheyne Walk; the painting is reproduced in *The Scenery of London*.

32 The painting (below) entitled *Old Men's Gardens at Chelsea Hospital*, is by Helen Allingham (a member of the Royal Watercolour Society) and was published in *Happy England* by A&C Black in 1903. The two other images of Chelsea pensioners (above and left) are from *Living London*, Volume 1; the image on the left shows the pensioners with their "black jacks," or leather drinking vessels.

33 Two paintings of exactly the same view of Emanuel Hospital, which was founded by Lady Dacre, sister of Thomas Sackville, Earl of Dorset. The first (right) is by Herbert Marshall from *The Scenery of London*. The other (below) is by Philip Norman; it was painted in 1890, two years before the hospital was closed.

34 The panorama of Trafalgar Square (below) dates from 1909. The other two images are photochromes showing Nelson's Column from slightly different angles.

35 *The Death of General Gordon* (below) on January 26, 1885, as depicted by G. W. Joy and reproduced in *Hutchinson's Story of the British Nation*. The portrait of Gordon (top right) is from the same source, and the photograph of Trafalgar Square shows the statue of Gordon in position before it was moved to Victoria Embankment Gardens in 1943.

36 The painting (left) shows a wedding in St. Paul's Kensington, and the book cover for *Modern Marriage* was reproduced in the *Penrose Pictorial Annual* of 1908–9. The portrait of Handel (right) is from *Hutchinson's Story of the British Nation*.

37 *He Staggered Forward and Reached the Landing* is the dramatic title of the drawing (left) that illustrated a children's story in *Chatterbox*, published by Wells Gardner & Co. Ltd. London in 1906. *What the Fireman Did* (center) illustrates a story from *The Child's Own Magazine*, Volume 22, published by W. Clowes and Sons in 1905. *The Fire Brigade Leaving Its Headquarters* (right) is from *Living London*, Volume 1.

38 The photograph of St. Mary le Strand (right) is from *The Old Churches of London*, published by Batsford in 1941. The colored image is by Nelson Dawson, as published in *A Wanderer in London* by Methuen & Co. in 1906.

39 The drawing (top right) shows children clustered around the same fountain in St. James's Park that Rose Barton featured in her painting. The photograph (below) was published in Volume 3 of *Living London*.

40 The fine painting of pelicans (top left) is by William Kuhnert and was published in *Harmsworth Natural History* in 1910. Two drakes pursuing a duck (top right) is from *The British Bird Book*, published in 1913, and the painting by Yoshio Markino (below), entitled *Feeding the Wildfowl in St James's Park*, was published in 1914 by Chatto & Windus.

41 The map showing Parliament Street is from *Bacon's Up-to-Date Pocket Atlas and Guide to London* of 1902, and the photo (below) shows Parliament Street today. Brunel (right) smokes his cigar in this well-known portrait.

42 The Royal Scots Greys 2nd Dragoons (right) are entering Horse Guards in this coronation procession from a coronation souvenir booklet produced with the compliments of R. W. Righton in 1902. The photochrome (left) shows the Horse Guards as published in *London in Colour Photography*.

43 A bottle seller outside St. Bartholomew's Hospital (top left), from *Living London*, Volume 2, made money from the fact that the hospital did not supply bottles (for medicines) to patients. Herbert Marshall painted St. Bartholomew's Square (below), as published in *The Scenery of London* in 1905. St Bartholomew's Hospital is visible on the left.

44 The drawing of the gateway of St. James's Palace (right) comes from *Walks in London*, Volume 2, by Augustus Hare, published by Daldy, Isbister and Co. in 1878. The central image is a photochrome, and the Oilette postcard (left) from a painting by Harry Payne shows the changing of the guard at Buckingham Palace—the Coldstream guards relieving the Grenadiers.

45 The mudlarks (top) are from *Living London*, Volume 1, as is the image of loaded barges at Bankside (right). The painting (left) of the Houses of Parliament from Lambeth is by Herbert Marshall from *The Scenery of London*.

46 The child asleep on the doorstep (right) appeared in the *Penrose Pictorial Annual* 1912–13 with the caption "Tired out." Hugh Thomson drew *A Doorstep Party* (left) in 1902, and the photograph (top) shows a ragged school union dinner in Camberwell as depicted in *Living London*, Volume 1.

47 A photochrome of the Victoria and Albert Museum (top), and two different views of the Natural History Museum in Kensington: one (left) from *Ryman's Handy Handbook of London*, and the other (right) from *401 views of London*.

48 St. James's Street from the New University Club is the setting for the painting (right) by Herbert Marshall, published in *The Scenery of London* in 1905. The painting of a levee at St. James's Palace (below left) is from *London's Social Calendar*. St. James's Street and St. James's Palace (top left) by Nelson Dawson comes from *A Wanderer in London*, published by Methuen & Co. in 1906.

49 Yoshio Markino painted Earls Court Station (below right), and the underground map (below left) dates from 1908. The railway map (far left) is from 1902, as published in *Bacon's Up-to-Date Atlas to London*. George Davy drew the "strap hangers" (top), which was reproduced as a comic postcard.

50 The advertisement for corsets available at Harrods (right) comes from *The Ladies' Field Magazine* of April 11, 1914. This magazine cost sixpence a week. The postcard (middle) shows Brompton Road. The lady shopper (left) was part of a design for a drapery catalog cover, as reproduced in the *Penrose Pictorial Annual* 1905–6.

51 The soldier's pass (right) was reproduced in the first volume of *Living London* in 1902. The painting of Constitution Hill (left) by Yoshio Markino was reproduced in *The Colour of London* in 1914.

52 Charing Cross Station from the river (below) by Herbert Marshall is from *The Scenery of London*. The photochrome (right) showing Charing Cross Station and the Strand was printed in *London in Colour Photography*.

53 The photograph (left) shows the interior of the Cheshire Cheese, and we see the Cheshire Cheese again in the Haslehust painting (below) of Wine Office Court and the Cheshire Cheese in Fleet Street, as published in *Beautiful London*. The drawing of Fleet Street (right) is an illustration from *London* by Walter Besant, first published in 1892.

54 The portrait of Kate Greenaway in her studio in 1895 (top) is from the A&C Black book *Kate Greenaway* by Spielmann and Layard, published in 1905. *Bubbles* is the title of the painting (middle) from *Rhymes for Young Folk*, as reproduced in the Spielmann and Layard book. Mortimer Menpes painted the Lilac Sunbonnet (below), which was printed in *World's Children*, published by A&C Black in 1903.

55 The photograph of Tottenham Court Road (left) is from *401 Views of London*. Two advertisements for Heals (below and right) show the range of chinaware available—the advertisement (below) is from *The Connoisseur: A Magazine for Collectors*, Volume 16, November 1906.

56 Two sentimental portraits of children from the *Penrose Pictorial Annual* of 1907–8: *Childhood* (top) and *Secrets* (left). *Taking in the Roses* is the title of the Kate Greenaway painting (below right).

57 Two drawings by Hugh Thomson—*The Bus Driver* (top left) and *Inside the Omnibus* (middle) from *Highways and Byways in London*, published in 1902. The orderly boy (right)—whose job was to dodge in and out of traffic to sweep up any refuse—appeared in *London in Colour Photography*. The advertisement for the omnibus appeared in *Motor Traction* of April 1906.

58 The drawing of St. Martin-in-the-Fields church (below center) appeared in *Ryman's Handy Handbook of London*. The misty view of Trafalgar Square (left) was painted by Yoshio Markino, and E. Haslehust painted the other view (top right).

59 Two paintings of the Old Bell Inn, Southwark, by Philip Norman (below) from *London Vanished and Vanishing*, published by A&C Black in 1905. The coffee room (below right) is the room that we can see under the lamp on the right-hand side of the painting of the yard of the Old Bell (left). Similar architecture is found in the painting of the remains of the George Inn, Southwark, by E. W. Haslehust (top), as reproduced in *Beautiful London*.

60 The photochrome of St. Martin-in-the-Fields church and the National Gallery (above) shows the same view as the two paintings (below) but from a slightly different angle. The paintings are both by Herbert Marshall, from *The Scenery of London*.

61 *River Steps, Waterloo Bridge* by E. W. Haslehust (top) emphasizes the grandeur of the architecture; Haslehust also painted *The Thames from Below Waterloo Bridge* (below), looking toward the city. Both were included in the forty-eight paintings in *Beautiful London*, published by Blackie and Son around 1909.

These notes refer to the map section on pages 146–161, describing the images around the edges of the maps reading from the top down. The numbers refer to the page numbers.

147 A map of Regents Park Zoo, from the 1907 *ABC 3d Guide to London*; elephant at the zoo, from *401 Views of London* published by W. H. Smith; *In the Lion-House at the Zoo*, painted by J. Williamson, from *The Children's Book of London* published by A&C Black in 1903; Lords Pavilion, from *London* by A. R. Hope Moncrieff, published by A&C Black in 1916.

148 Passengers gathered at Euston Station, from *Living London*, Volume 1; Regents Park, from *Living London*, Volume 1; University College Gower Street, from *401 Views of London*.

149 A third-class ticket from Bradford to Kings Cross via Carcroft, which cost 15 shillings 10 and half pence; Kings Cross Station and St. Pancras Station, both from *401 Views of London*; the Foundling Hospital in Guildford Street, which provided a home for 550 children in the early 1900s, from *Living London*, Volume 1.

150 Wesley's Chapel, City Road; the interior of Wesley's Chapel; Bunyan's Grave, Bunhill Fields, City Road. All images from *401 Views of London*.

151 The Bethnal Green Museum; Head Quarters of the Honourable Artillery Company, City Road; Finsbury Square. All images from *401 Views of London*.

152 A Great Western Railway ticket costing 1 shilling, sixpence from Paddington to any Great Western destination not exceeding 75 miles from Paddington; children sailing boats at the Round Pond in Kensington Gardens, from *401 Views of London*; a photochrome of the Dutch Garden in Kensington Palace, published in *London in Colour Photography*; skating on the Serpentine, from *Living London*, Volume 2.

153 A photochrome of Marble Arch from *London in Colour Photography*; Kensington High Street from *401 Views of London*; the Albert Memorial from *London in Colour Photography*.

154 The British Museum, from *London in Colour Photography*; a photochrome of the law courts in the Strand; the Savoy Hotel, from *Penrose Pictorial Annual* of 1905–6.

155 The Thames Embankment, from the *Penrose Pictorial Annual* of 1904–5; a photochrome of Westminster Abbey, from *London in Colour Photography*, published by the London Photochrom Company; Westminster Bridge and Saint Thomas's Hospital, from *London in Colour Photography*.

156 St. Paul's Cathedral, from *London in Colour Photography*; an etching of a view of London across the Thames, from *Penrose Pictorial Annual* of 1912–13; London Bridge and the Monument, from *London in Colour Photography*.

157 The White Tower of London, from *London in Colour Photography*; St. Katherine's Dock in 1828, from a booklet published by the Port of London Authority in March 1914; the Port of London flags, from the back cover of the same booklet.

158 Chelsea Church painted by Yoshio Markino and published in *A Japanese Artist in London* by Chatto & Windus in 1910; Brompton Road, from *401 Views of London*; Brompton Oratory, from the same source.

159 Chelsea Hospital, from *Living London*, Volume 1; Chelsea Staith painted by Herbert Marshall, from *The Scenery of London*; Battersea Park, from *401 Views of London*.

160 Westminster Cathedral, from *London in Colour Photography*; Victoria Station in 1900; the Tate Gallery, from *London in Colour Photography*.

161 A photochrome of Lambeth Palace; two images of the Oval Cricket Ground, from *Living London*, Volume 2.

BIBLIOGRAPHY

The ABC Guide to London, distributed by Chas Baker & Co's Stores Ltd, 1907 and 1916.

Bacon's Up-to-Date Pocket Atlas and Guide to London, G.W. Bacon and Co. Ltd, 1902.

Beautiful London, text by Walter Jerrold with 48 paintings by E. W. Haslehust, Blackie and Son Ltd.

Chatterbox, founded by J. Erskine Clarke, Wells Gardner, Darton & Co, 1906.

The Children's Book of London, G. E. Milton, A&C Black, 1903.

The Child's Own Magazine, printed by William Clowes and Son, 1905.

Chronicles of London, C. L. Kingsford, Clarendon Press, 1905.

Collecting Postcards, William Dûval with Valerie Monahan, Blandford Press, 1978.

The Colour of London, W. J. Loftie, paintings by Yoshio Markino, Chatto and Windus, 1914.

Colour Printing and Colour Printers, R. M. Burch, Pitman & Sons Ltd, 1910.

The Connoisseur: A Magazine for Collectors, Otto Ltd, Carmelite House.

Cook's Handbook for London, 1904, 1905, 1906, Thomas Cook & Son.

The Dictionary of British Watercolour Artists up to 1920, Volume 1, Huon Mallalieu, Antique Collectors' Club.

Discovering London Plaques, Derek Sumeray, Shire, 1999.

The Early History of Piccadilly, Leicester Square, Soho and their Neighbourhoods, C. L. Kinsford, Cambridge University Press, 1925.

Edwardian Fashion, Pauline Stevenson, Ian Allan Ltd, 1980.

Edwardian Life and Leisure, Ronald Pearsall, David and Charles, 1973.

The Edwardians, Roy Hattersley, Little, Brown, 2004.

Edwardian Theatre, A. E. Wilson, Baker, 1951.

England, Frank Fox, A&C Black, 1918.

401 Views of London, W.H. Smith & Son.

The Gardener's Assistant, Robert Thompson, edited by William Watson, Volumes 1–3, Gresham Publishing Company, 1900.

Happy England, Helen Allingham, A&C Black, 1903.

Harmsworth Natural History, Volumes 1–3, Carmelite House, 1910.

Highways and Byways in London, Mrs. E. T. Cook, with illustrations by Hugh Thomson and F. L. Griggs, Macmillan and Co Ltd, 1902.

A History of London Transport, Theodore Barker and Richard Robbins, George Allen & Unwin, 1963.

A History of Shopping, Dorothy Davis, Routledge & Kegan Paul, 1966.

Hutchinson's Story of the British Nation, Volumes 1–4, Hutchinson & Co.

A Japanese Artist in London, Yoshio Markino, Chatto and Windus, 1910.

Kate Greenaway, M. H. Spielmann and G. S. Layard, A&C Black, 1905.

The Kings and Queens of England, Sir George Bellow, a companion book to *The Royal Line of Succession*, Patrick W. Montague-Smith, Debrett.

The Ladies' Field Magazine, April 11, 1914, Volume LXV, No. 839.

Living London, edited by George R. Sims, Volumes 1–3, Cassell and Co Ltd, 1902–3.

London, A. R. Hope Mancrieff, A&C Black, 1916.

London, Walter Besant, Chatto and Windus, 1904.

London, A Sketch Book, L. G. Hornby, A&C Black, 1912.

London, the Port of the Empire, Port of London Authority, 1914.

London Alleys, Byways and Courts, drawn and described by Alan Stapleton, John Lane and the Bodley Head Ltd, 1924.

London in Colour Photography, Foreword by George R. Sims, London Photocrom Company Limited.

The London Encyclopaedia, edited by Ben Weinreb and Christopher Hibbert, Macmillan, 1983.

London and Its Environs, Handbook for Travellers, Karl Baedeker, Baedeker, 1911.

London 1900, Jonathan Schneer, Yale University Press, 1999.

London in the Nineteenth Century, Walter Besant, A&C Black, 1909.

London's Social Calendar, the Savoy Hotel, c. 1910.

London of Today, edited by C. E. Pascoe, 1895–97.

The London Tramcar 1861–1952, R. W. Kidner, Oakwood Press, 1970.

London Vanished and Vanishing, painted and described by Philip Norman, A&C Black, 1905.

Lost London, E. B. Chancellor, Constable, 1926.

The Making of Modern London 1815–1914, Gavin Weightman and Steve Humphries, Sidgwick and Jackson, 1984.

Motor Buses in London 1904–8, R. W. Kidner, Oakwood Press, 1975.

The Old Churches of England, Gerald Cobb, B.T. Batsford Ltd, 1941.

Olivia's Shopping and How She Does It: A Prejudiced Guide to the London Shops, Gay and Bird, 1905.

Our Darlings, edited by Dr. Barnado, John F. Shaw and Co Ltd, annual.

Penrose's Pictorial Annual, 1901–1915, edited by William Gamble, Penrose and Co.

Peter Pan in Kensington Gardens, retold by May Byron, illustrated by Arthur Rackham, Hodder and Stoughton Ltd.

The Picture Postcards of Raphael Tuck and Sons, J. H. D. Smith, IPM, Colchester, 2000.

Philips' Handy Volume Atlas of the County of London, George Philip and Son Ltd, 1902.

Ryman's Handy Handbook of London, George Falkner and Sons.

The Scenery of London, painted by Herbert M. Marshall, described by G. E. Mitton, A&C Black, 1905.

Souvenir of the Coronation of King Edward VII, with the compliments of R. W. Righton, Wholesale, Retail and General Draper, Manchester House, Evesham, 1902.

The Thames, Jonathan Schneer, Little, Brown, 2005.

Toys, Dolls, Games: Paris 1903–1914, Denys Ingram, 1981.

Walks in London, Volume 2, Augustus J. C. Hare, Daldy Isbister and Co. 1878.

A Wanderer in London, E. V. Lucas, iIllustrated by Nelson Dawson, Methuen & Co, 1906.

Wayside and Woodland Blossoms, Edward Step, illustrated by Mabel E. Step, Frederick Warne & Co, 1909.

World's Children, Mortimer Menpes, text by Dorothy Menpes A&C Black, 1903.

A City Policeman, from *London in Colour Photography*

THE TIMES PAST ARCHIVE

The Memories of Times Past series would be inconceivable without the massive Times Past Archive, a treasury of books, magazines, atlases, postcards, and printed ephemera from the golden age of color printing between 1895 and 1915.

From the time several years ago when the project was first conceived, the collecting of material from all over the world has proceeded in earnest. As well as a complete set of the ninety-two A&C Black 20 Shilling color books, which are the inspiration for the series, the archive houses full sets of period *Baedeker* and *Murray's Guides*; almost every color-illustrated travel book from illustrious publishing houses like Dent, Jack, Cassell, Blackie, and Chatto & Windus; and a massive collection of reference works with color plates on subjects from railways and military uniforms to wildflowers and birds' eggs.

The archive also contains complete runs of all the important periodicals of the time that contained color illustrations, including the pioneering *Penrose's Pictorial Annual: An Illustrated Review of the Graphic Arts*; the first-ever British color magazine, *Colour*; ladies' magazines like *Ladies' Field* and *The Crown*; and more popular titles such as *The Connoisseur* and *The London Magazine*.

These years were vintage years for atlas publishing, and the Times Past Archive contains such gems as Keith Johnston's *Royal Atlas of Modern Geography*, *The Harmsworth Atlas*, Bartholomew's *Survey Atlas of England and Wales*, and the *Illustrated and Descriptive Atlas of the British Empire*.

Last but not least, the archive includes a wealth of smaller items—souvenirs, postcards, tickets, programs, catalogs, posters, and all the colorful ephemera with which the readers of the original 20 Shilling books would have been familiar.

THE TIMES PAST WEB SITE

The Web site to accompany this project can be found at www.memoriesoftimespast.com, where you will find further information about the birth and development of the project, together with the complete original texts of titles published to date. There is also an area where you can take part in discussions raised by readers of the books who want to take their interest further and share their memories and passions with others. The Web site will start small and elegant, as you would expect of an "Edwardian Web site," but it will gradually become what you and we together make it, a place for devotees of art and culture from a century ago to meet and be inspired.

Every effort has been made to ensure the accuracy of the information presented in this book. The publisher will not assume liability for damages caused by inaccuracies in the data and makes no warranty whatsoever expressed or implied. The publisher welcomes comments and corrections from readers, which will be incorporated in future editions; e-mail can be sent to corrections@memoriesoftimespast.com.

ILLUSTRATION CREDITS

l = left, r = right, b = bottom, t = top, m = middle
Page references refer to pages in this title.

Collecting Postcards, William Dûval with Valerie Monahan, Blandford Press 1978, page 14(bl), plate 44(l), plate 49(t);
The Dictionary of British Watercolour Artists up to 1920, Volume 1, Huon Mallalieu, Antique Collectors' Club, page 22(l);
David and Jonathan Downes, page 21(t, r, and br)
Don Kurtz via www.artrenewal.org, page 19(r);
Edwardian Fashion, Pauline Stevenson, Ian Allan Ltd, 1980, plate 16(br);

The London Transport Museum, page 160(m);
Motor Buses in London 1904–8, R. W. Kidner, Oakwood Press, 1975, plate 57(bl);
The Picture Postcards of Raphael Tuck and Sons, J. H. D. Smith, IPM, Colchester, plate 13(tl), page 167(t and r);
Toys, Dolls, Games: Paris 1903–1914, Denys Ingram, 1981, plate 14(br);
www.artrenewal.org, page 20(tr), page 21 (bl), page 23 (l and r);
www.mooseyscountrygarden.com, plate 30(r).

The authors would like to thank Christopher Pick for his contribution to several plate captions.

The Porch of the Carlton Hotel at Night, painted by Yoshio Markino, from *The Colour of London*, 1914